Relationship

Paul Evanson & Dana Keller

Copyright © 2013 Paul Evanson & Dana Keller

All rights reserved.

ISBN: 0989235904

ISBN-13: 978-0-9892359-0-7

CONTENTS

Foreword	viii
Introduction	1
Part 1 – Living in Authentic Relationship	5
Chapter 1: The Meaning of Life	7
Chapter 2: Reprioritizing	12
Chapter 3: One Interaction at a Time	17
Chapter 4: It's Not About You	21
Chapter 5: It's All About You	25
Chapter 6: Summary of Part 1	29
Part 2 – Relationship Applied	30
Chapter 7: The Power of Relationship by John Bateman	31

CONTENTS

Chapter 8: Relationship Within Boundaries: Just Say No to Carpooling by Dana Keller	50
Chapter 9: Relationship in the Workplace: Lessons in Leadership from the Military by Mark Ammons	55
Chapter 10: Relationships in the Family of God by Casey Peterson	70
Chapter 11: Relationship and Addiction by Heather Larson	77
Part 3 – Pressing on: One Interaction at a Time	96
Chapter 12: How Will Care be Delivered? A conversation with Steve Mason	98
Chapter 13: The Relational Church by Dave Browning	117
Afterthought: Being Loved	130
Acknowledgements	132
Contact Information	135

FOREWORD

You may not have time to read this book. With a million other things in life pulling our attentions this way and that—some of them quite real and valuable, like families, jobs, and health, and others maybe not so much—you may not have the time or energy for one more thing. Regardless of which direction or how many you're being pulled in, it is true that you must choose to spend your time with the awareness and behaviors presented in this book.

Perhaps you already know that:

- God created you for an intimate, loving relationship with Him.

- This relationship with God is only made complete when we love others.

- We build this relationship one interaction at a time.

And, knowing this, you live your life in a way that shows:

- Nothing is more important.

- Everything else is details.

- We are not meant to do this alone.

Relationship

If you already know these things and live your life in a way that shows it, maybe your time will be better spent somewhere else. But, if, like us and many people we know, you have been living your life doing a million things—having many friendships, building a loving marriage, creating a successful career, serving in your church community—and yet have an inexplicable emptiness or sadness…then maybe, just maybe God will help alleviate that through this book.

We have been there and done that and we are not "there" yet, because there is no "there" in this life. But we chose to begin the journey and are much better off for it. We will share with you what God has shared with us, and perhaps it is time for you to choose to begin as well.

Blessings!

Paul and Dana

INTRODUCTION

You are not alone.

You never have been alone.

Your maker did not create and then discard you. Every hair on your head has been numbered by him. He will always be with you because He loves you.

I do not want to minimize the deep, painful loneliness you may have experienced or are experiencing. It's real because you feel it and loneliness impacts your daily behaviors and ultimately the quality of your life. The debilitating weight of loneliness can make life seem pointless and simply not worth living. You feel irrelevant.

Relationship begets relevance. Who am I? Why am I here? What is my purpose? What is important to me? All of these questions and more are answered through relationship.

We were not meant to live this life alone.

Despite what our culture may tell us, we were not designed to travel through life on earth as independent individuals, succeeding or failing, living and dying by our own strength and wits. People have tried to live their lives this way over centuries of human existence and the result, either inwardly, outwardly or both is always the same—impotence at best and wreckage and ruin at worst.

In His grand design our maker built us with sustenance requirements: air, water, food, shelter, warmth and relationship. Without any one of these we will die. Without air we are good for 3-5 minutes before we begin to die. We can live several days without water before death becomes imminent.

In the same way, when we are deprived of relationship, we begin to die a long, painful death that happens over not minutes or days, but years. The physical, biological and spiritual laws that govern God's creation are already set in place and determine the timing, cause and effect of our lives.

The kind of relationship God wants with and for us is honest and intimate. He wants us to be in authentic relationships with those around us regardless if it's a 30-second encounter or one that lasts a lifetime. This kind of relationship is not based on quantity but on quality.

Most of us are starving for authentic relationship. Many people are surrounded by family and friends yet still feel alone and empty. Overcome by our hunger we will resort to anything to meet our need. We'll "dumpster dive" in any low place where there might be a hint of relationship. We'll forego other needs like self-respect and integrity to fulfill our relationship hunger yet we find ourselves feeling emptier and even more alone.

Physical starvation occurs in three stages. The first and second are characterized first by discomfort and then pain as the body metabolizes any and all reserves. During these first two stages a person will exchange rational, "civilized" behavior and thought in order to meet their growing need.

In the third and final stage of starvation, however, a person becomes listless, apathetic and withdrawn as their body literally devours its own muscles and vital proteins. Paradoxically, as starvation increases the ability of the body to consume normal volumes of food decreases.

In much the same way, most of us are starving for connection with others yet outwardly appear to be calm, "together" and even happy despite our internal pain and discomfort. The ability to receive love becomes muted. It is only occasionally that someone is so completely starved for authentic relationship that we see their pain because their depression and anxiety have become debilitating. Many times their outward suffering makes us feel uncomfortable and instead of reaching out in an authentic way, we give advice like "pull yourself up by your bootstraps" or "just try to think more positively" or even "I'll be praying for you" without taking the time to give them the real connection that they are starving for.

So whose fault is this? Where is this God and why doesn't He help us?

There is nothing good that God doesn't want you to have. In fact, He has great plans for you.

We are on a journey to become honest, authentic human beings and some of us are going to make it. Others will not.

This universe was created to operate in a specific way, governed by both natural and spiritual laws. To achieve the life God intended for you, you must learn and adapt to those laws. You must take the first step of your journey.

About this book

This book is written in three parts. Part One is an explanation of relationship. It reflects our understanding of what God wants for us during our time on this planet. We collaborated on the content, learning from our experiences of broken ways of operating in our own lives.

Part Two was also written in relationship with others. Each chapter, written by individual contributors, tells a story of relationship played out in the writer's life.

Though the principles of relationship are simple, they are not easy to apply and these are stories of how relationship or lack thereof has impacted real lives. We think you will find something to relate to in each of the stories in this part of the book.

Part Three contains thoughts on the implications for the Church if indeed our primary purpose is to live in relationship. Many of us are thirsting for real community in our places of worship, and churches-despite their best efforts-are coming up short. Two people who have served the Church for many years reflect on the current state of the Church and how we may move forward to truly serve one another, in love.

Relationship is both the beginning point and final destination for your journey. Our hope is that you will fully realize and experience the wonderful, unspeakable bounty God has for you.

PART 1–LIVING IN AUTHENTIC RELATIONSHIP

Before all things existed there was relationship. Before time itself the triune God, three distinct personalities in one being, lived in beautiful, pure and complete intimacy. The Three-in-One knew and loved each other completely. Creation was an act of that relationship. After speaking the stars, planets, animals, plants and all other matter into being they said, "Let us make man in our image."

"Then God said, "Let us make man in our image, in our likeness, and let them rule over the fish of the sea and the birds of the air, over the livestock, over all the earth, and over all the creatures that move along the ground." Genesis 1:26

This act of love produced man who was, himself, a combination of body, mind and spirit. One man with multiple facets. But God knew that the creation process was not complete.

"The Lord God said, 'It is not good for the man to be alone." Genesis 2:18

Adam needed a mate. The couple needed a family. The family needed friends. God met these needs; Adam did not.

Since that time we have individually existed in a trinity of relationship: ourselves, God and others. History is nothing more than a record of relationships and the consequences of those relationships.

Paul Evanson & Dana Keller

Having trouble understanding the past? Examine past relationships. Having troubles today? Examine your current relationships with God and others. The answers are found there. Everything else follows.

CHAPTER 1: THE MEANING OF LIFE

Why are you here? What is the purpose of your life?

Jesus told us straight out what our mission is:

"And one of them, an expert in religious law, asked him a question to test him: 'Teacher, which commandment in the law is the greatest?' Jesus said to him, 'Love the Lord your God with all your heart, with all your soul, and with all your mind.' This is the first and greatest commandment. The second is like it: 'Love your neighbor as yourself.' All the law and the prophets depend on these two commandments."
Matthew 22:35-40

Other translations say, *"All the law and the prophets hang on these two commandments."*

We search for life's meaning but Jesus has already told us what it is: our relationship with God and our relationship with others. Begin here. Focus on it. Meditate on it. Open your ears and heart and allow the Holy Spirit to teach you about it. If you go anywhere, go here. If you can't go here, don't go anywhere. Nothing else matters in comparison.

"Love the Lord your God with all your heart, with all your soul and with all your mind. This is the first and greatest commandment."

God is only asking one primary thing from you: "Love me completely." Your relationship with God is your purpose, the reason you are alive. To have a robust, intimate, evolving relationship with God is your reason for being. When you give a higher priority to anything else, you lose. Who really cares what you have accomplished if you haven't fulfilled the greatest commandment? Not God. Not your mate. Not your family. Not your authentic friends.

Yet, for many who are raised in a church or faith tradition, there is a long list of "shoulds" that make up "being a good Christian." Reading the Bible, attending Bible studies, volunteering at church, participating in prayer groups, etc., and still the Church is filled with people who don't really know God.

Is God some remote deity who wants you to do x, y, and z to be in his good graces? Do you talk to Him in an intimate way or only when you need something? I think it's worth asking yourself how you can love God with "all your heart, all your soul and all your mind." How does that look different than what your relationship is like now?

What are some expressions of a healthy relationship?

- You look forward to your time with the other person.
- No secrets. You feel free to tell her anything. Nothing is hidden.
- You look forward to hearing what he has to say.
- You accept the other person as they are and feel accepted in return.
- You think about him regularly and wonder how he is doing.
- You communicate regularly.

How much are you supposed to love God? With your whole heart, as if nothing matters more. And it doesn't. Nothing matters more.

One of the things that keeps us apart from God is judgment—or perhaps misjudgment is a better term. Since we ate from the

Relationship

Tree of Knowledge of Good and Evil we have used what we think we know to incorrectly judge ourselves and others and, at times, even God.

"Knowledge puffs up, but love builds up. The man who thinks he knows something does not yet know as he ought to know. But the man who loves God is known by God." 1 Corinthians 8:1-3

We think we know what being a good Christian looks like, what being a good parent is, what being healthy is, who God is and how He works--but we really don't know. Our thinking is pushed and pulled by our culture, our egos, our upbringing and every aspect of the earthly world and then we use that false knowledge to compare ourselves and negatively judge ourselves and others.

"She's not a good Christian." "God would never do that." "He's a terrible father." These false perceptions and comparisons keep us from having the kind of authentic relationship God wants with us. We are so focused on "doing it right"according to what we know that we're missing the point. We don't know. God does.

"And I pray that you, being rooted and established in love, may have power, together with all the saints, to grasp how wide and long and high and deep is the love of Christ, and to know this love that surpasses knowledge—that you may be filled to the measure of all the fullness of God." Ephesians 3:17-19

God can't be put into a neat package that our minds can comprehend. The creator of the universe, designer of all life, cannot be fully understood by our limited human mind. Our job is not to try to figure out why God wants what he wants. Our job is to talk to Him, rely on Him, trust Him, be honest with Him, and spend time with Him--all the things we want from any other authentic relationship.

"Love your neighbor as yourself."

We were not meant to live our lives alone. Your purpose is not complete unless you are in relationship with others. We were not meant to sit in conversation with God alone all day, every day, nor were we created to live out a solitary life focusing on our outer appearance while our innermost needs remain unexpressed and unmet. Shame, fear, depression, denial and anxiety are only a few symptoms of those unmet needs. They are warning signs that we are focused on earthly things instead of on our relationship with God and with others.

Though I don't claim to understand it, I must admit it: In order to experience the fullness of life we need each other on a consistent basis and at an intimate level. The better my relationship with God, the more I start to see people through His eyes. It makes me want to 1) be the best I can be for them and 2) stay out of the way so He can be in relationship with them through me.

In India, the common greeting between people is "Namaste", which roughly translated means, "the perfect light in me sees the perfect light in you." When we see the "perfect light" of God in each other, in every interaction, we start to fulfill our purpose. While this may sound like a challenging task, it helps to remember that we're not on our own with this one. The Holy Spirit is always there. In Matthew 18:20, God tells us *"For where two or three come together in my name, there I am with them."* That means that every conversation is a three-way conversation—between you, the other person, and the Holy Spirit.

When I say we need to approach "every interaction" by trying to see God in the other person, I really mean <u>every</u> interaction. We need to have God's perspective, not just when we are with our close friends and family members, but also with the man at the bus stop, the co-worker in our office, the cashier at the coffee bar, the server at the restaurant—

everyone we meet. Even a ten-second interaction can be life changing, not because we did anything, but because the Holy Spirit worked through us to reveal something to the other person. That can only happen when we are fully present and mindful of God's presence as well.

This is your primary reason for being.

CHAPTER 2: REPRIORITIZING

You have one primary purpose: Love God, Love your neighbor in every interaction every day you are on this planet. Only you can fulfill this purpose. Accomplishing this requires two things:

1. Loving God and loving your neighbor becomes your priority.
2. Making relationships with others the priority in every area of your life.

Our standard priorities lose meaning in light of this. How many people do you know that would say they "know" God? If you belong to a church community, probably every single one of them. They might think that their busy lives demonstrate how well they know God. They may even be "winning souls for Christ" through mission work or sharing their testimony with others. But do they have an intimacy with God that surpasses all other relationships? Now, I'm not saying there is anything wrong with any of the above activities. What I am saying is that knowing God is about much more than going through the motions that we think demonstrate our knowledge of Him. If we are going to make loving God our main concern—and we must if we are to live in the kind of authentic relationship He planned for us—then we have to make our relationship with Him our number one priority.

As we said earlier, to know God means spending time with Him. Listening to Him. Being aware of His presence, of His desire for you. Treating Him like you would your best friend. When we do these things, read His word, and strive to see God in every person we meet, that's when we truly get to know

Relationship

Him. When our relationship with God is in the forefront of our minds every day, then we can't help but love ourselves and our neighbor. Knowing Him is the foundation of living a life in authentic relationship and everything else flows from that.

Our achievement-oriented culture makes it easy for us to lose sight of this. In the documentary, "Happy", the filmmaker illustrates how detrimental it is to our own sense of happiness when we value achievement over relationship. One story, set in Japan, one of the most achievement-oriented cultures in the world, focuses on people who are actually dying from overwork and lack of genuine relationships. They have a name for it: "Karoshi".

Without food, air, and water, we die. Without relationship, we die. God did not design us as human "doings." All of our achievements and hard work are fine for this world but they are not our purpose. Work, school, family, and community are all there to provide us with one thing: the opportunity to be in authentic relationship with others. Everything we are involved in is simply a context in which we can connect with other people through the Holy Spirit. Authentic relationship is the only thing that will fill the hole of loneliness that cripples us and, in some cases, kills us.

Even though authentic relationships are sometimes challenging, especially when we're dealing with difficult people or situations, or when we've never experinced healthy relationships, God is there to lighten our load. In Matthew 11:28-30 he tells us:

"Come to me all you who are weary and burdened and I will give you rest. Take my yoke upon you and learn from me, for I am gentle and humble in heart, and you will find rest for your souls. For my yoke is easy and my burden is light."

When we recognize that the Holy Spirit is present and let God do the heavy lifting, life is much less difficult than it otherwise

would be! There is a joke that goes:
What's the difference between you and God? God doesn't pretend to be you.

We don't have to try to be in control of anything. God's got it covered. Sure, living life this way doesn't happen overnight. The good news—no the great news—is that God gives us opportunities to practice every day. We don't have to be great at having authentic exchanges right away; God allows us to practice, one interaction at a time.

This past Christmas season my daughter and I spent a day together shopping. For me it was just so much fun to be with her and each of the shopkeepers, waitresses and cashiers we met. At the end of the day she told me, "Dad, people just love you. I don't know how you do it." It was an opportunity for me to share what I'm learning and to explain God's role in it. There is nothing better than seeing love in action and I'm so grateful my daughter got to witness it first hand.

In every interaction, we have the opportunity to create an authentic relationship whether it's with someone we've known 10 seconds or someone we've known 10 years. With each person we meet, we can allow God to participate. In order for the other person to connect with Him through us, we must give up any selfish priorities. When people meet you, are they experiencing God or your ego? Is His plan or yours at work in the conversation? His plan is always better.

What are some of the things we normally prioritize in interactions with others?

- being right
- getting our way
- being efficient
- getting things done
- getting something we need
- providing a service

Relationship

Once we recognize that there is a goal far beyond the worldly reason for our interaction every conversation is elevated to a heavenly purpose. We may or may not ever see or understand what God accomplished but, if we trust that He is there and using us, then we have done what we're supposed to do. Interacting in this way means we put all of those other priorities on the back burner and have one priority: love God, love your neighbor

By making our own immediate and worldly priorities second to this command, we are fulfilling God's purpose in every interaction.

Start ordering your day in light of this simple truth. When you look at what's important, make sure it's "who, not what." As you're making decisions, put the "who" first. The "what's" are what get us off track.

- Who is with me?
- Who is affected?
- Who is involved?
- Who does this matter to?

There is really no such thing as a "random interaction." Each human encounter has a reason.

How many times do we just go through the motions of our day? We get up, get the kids off to school, go to work, clean the house, do the shopping, go to church—often without having an authentic conversation the entire day.

Making relationships a priority means taking the time to be present. It means being aware of the people with whom we're interacting and taking the time to really see them, really listen to them. Rather than averting our eyes in line at the grocery store, it means engaging others in conversation. Many of those seemingly random people you encounter are feeling isolated, alone and unhappy. One small gesture—a quick smile, a light conversation, a compliment, sharing a joke—can change all that.

It can be scary to reach out to others. In fact, at first, some people might look at you like you're from another planet! But soon you'll find that you are demonstrating Christ's love in the world. You will be changing lives, one interaction at a time.

"This is my command—be strong and courageous! Do not be afraid or discouraged. For the Lord your God is with you wherever you go." Joshua 1:9

CHAPTER 3:
ONE INTERACTION
AT A TIME

Think about the interactions you've had so far today. What was said? How did the other person seem to be feeling? Did you look him or her in the eye? Did you pause long enough to be fully present? Did you ask God, "What do you want to do in this interaction?"

The only way we can do this work is by being fully present in every interaction. It is so easy to get bogged down in the past(accomplishment, shame, and regret) or to live in the future(worry, fear, and anxiety). But the past and future exist only in our thoughts. All that really exists is right here, right now—this moment.

So this moment is where we must practice. "Here I am, in the presence of this person(or people). God loves this person completely. How can I get out of the way and let God express Himself?"

It is so easy to go through our days numb and blind: to just give the cashier our money without looking her in the eye or talking to her, to kiss our spouse goodbye and go on about our day, to check our e-mails while listening to a friend on the phone. Our bodies are in one place but our minds are somewhere else. We are going through the motions.

Technology has only made things worse. All of our gadgets and 24/7 connection to information and entertainment pull us in multiple directions. While we are more "connected" than ever, people feel less connected and more alienated than ever. How many times have you been eating out and seen a couple with one person talking on their cell phone or furiously texting away? How many of us talk on the phone and drive? Technology is not bad in and of itself but when we don't pay attention to how we use it, it can serve as a wedge to keep us from being present. Technology seems to make us think that we can multi-task well but research has shown that we can't. God designed our brains to do one thing well at a time.

("Is Multitasking Bad for Us?" [http://www.pbs.org/wgbh/nova/body/is-multi- tasking-bad.html] by Brandon Keim, Nova Magazine, Oct 4, 2012);

It's amazing how much we've become used to the idea that we can multitask. For a day(or an hour!) challenge yourself—try doing one thing at a time. Try being fully present to the task at hand and, most importantly, to the people with whom you are interacting. We need to take inventory of anything that is distracting us from being present and make a plan to reduce or eliminate those distractions.

How Are We Doing?
Awareness is the first step, practice is the second, and evaluation and improvement is the third. God gives us great guidelines to figure out how we are doing. While the Bible is full of guidelines on how to be in authentic relationship, two come to mind.

The first is Galations 5:22: *"But the fruit of the Spirit is love, joy, peace, patience, kindness, goodness, faithfulness, gentleness and self-control. Against such things there is no law."*

Relationship

In our daily conversations with God, we can ask Him, "So, how am I doing on this?" and "Show me how I can improve." Chances are, if you pray for God to help you with love, joy, etc., he'll provide plenty of chances to practice. God is great that way.

The second verse that helps us determine how we are doing at being in authentic relationship is 1 Corinthians 13:4-8.

"Love is patient, love is kind. It does not envy, it does not boast, it is not proud. It is not rude, it is not self-seeking, it is not easily angered, it keeps no record of wrongs. Love does not delight in evil but rejoices with the truth. It always protects, always trusts, always hopes, always perseveres. Love never fails."

Since our purpose here is to love God, our neighbor, and ourselves, this verse a great self-evaluation tool and easy to apply every day.

- Was I patient? Was I kind?
- When I spoke to my friend was I envious or boastful?
- Did my pride get in the way?
- In what ways was I rude or self-seeking today?
- Did I lose my temper?
- Am I being forgiving or am I holding grudges?
- Was I honest in all my interactions? Did I secretly feel good about someone else's failure?
- How did I show that I am protecting and trusting with everyone I spoke to today?
- Did I hold back my own secrets in order to look good?

Love never fails. No matter what your answers are to any of these questions, if you focus on your purpose, love, you can't fail!

The answers to the questions above tell us how we can learn and grow and it is not done by trying harder. It's done by trying less and letting God do the heavy lifting. We just need to get out of His way and he'll shape us and the other person. Every interaction will be imperfect since we are imperfect beings. It's not a matter of our "doing it right." Any effort we make in being fully present and letting the Lord work through us is good effort.

Now What?

You may be overwhelmed at this point. "I certainly can't live up to these standards and I don't know anyone who can." Answer: God can. He has designed us to love Him and others by His love, his faith, his strength and his faithfulness. Our faith isn't even the size of a mustard seed or we'd be moving mountains! God's faith, on the other hand, is great.

"Have I not commanded you? Be strong and courageous. Do not be terrified; do not be discouraged, for the LORD your God will be with you wherever you go." Josh 1:9

"No temptation has seized you except what is common to man. And God is faithful; he will not let you be tempted beyond what you can bear. But when you are tempted, he will also provide a way out so that you can stand up under it." 1 Cor 10:13

"Do not be anxious about anything, but in every situation, by prayer and petition, with thanksgiving, present your requests to God." Philippians 4:5-7

That's it. You've begun by taking the first step on your journey. You didn't choose to begin? Nope. God chose for you to first be aware and then to begin your new journey. Today you can interact with God and you can most certainly interact with others. You know the answer. What you choose to do with it is up to you.

CHAPTER 4: IT'S NOT ABOUT YOU

*9 Two are better than one,
because they have a good return for their labor:*

*[10] If either of them falls down,
one can help the other up.
But pity anyone who falls
and has no one to help them up.*

*[11] Also, if two lie down together, they will keep warm.
But how can one keep warm alone?*

*[12] Though one may be overpowered,
two can defend themselves.*

A cord of three strands is not quickly broken.

Ecclesiastes 4:9-12

The notion that our purpose is love and that we need to be loving in every interaction, every day can seem daunting. God gave us free will. In the beginning we exercised that will by eating from the Tree of Knowledge of Good and Evil. The moment we did that we created a separation between ourselves and God and between ourselves and each other. Knowing became a separate action from being. In other words, we don't always do what we know is right.

We know how we should eat to be healthy but our actions don't always reflect that. We know how we need to manage our finances or that we should be taking care of the less fortunate but our knowing isn't always reflected in our actions. We have a choice.

We can choose to practice being in God's presence and getting out of His way so that he can use us fully. When we practice this in every interaction we have, then everyone we meet can experience God's love. How awesome is that? Even better, while we can practice, we never will be nor do we need to be perfect at it! God will make it into perfection. How great is it to know that we can take on a new way of being in the world and we cannot fail? Though we shouldn't fear failure, it is also true that we cannot do this alone.

- "But I'm good with people." You cannot do this alone.
- "But I volunteer my time to good causes." You cannot do this alone.
- "But I'm strong and smart." You cannot do this alone.

Only with God's strength can we fulfill our purpose.

"But the Lord stood at my side and gave me strength, so that through me the message might be fully proclaimed and all the Gentiles might hear it. And I was delivered from the lion's mouth." 2 Timothy 4:17

"So do not fear for I am with you, do not be dismayed, for I am your God. I will strengthen you and help you; I will uphold you with my righteous right hand." Isaiah 41:10

Your ability to love God with all your heart, mind, soul and strength and your neighbor as yourself is not about you. Your strengths and weaknesses, intelligence, past accomplishments or willpower are inconsequential. God will use you as He sees fit. Our choice is whether or not we want to cooperate with Him. Do we want to participate in the process? Do we want

Relationship

to experience the fullness of God's love through the work of the Holy Spirit? When we choose to engage with God, we participate in God's ability to work through us. As your relationship with Him grows you will inevitably begin to recognize His love for you and those around you. As you get to know Him more and more, it won't be hard work. You will look forward to the opportunity to love your neighbor. Why? Because He does.

Maybe you're thinking: "How could God use me? I'm too quiet or shy. I could never reach out to others." No matter how introverted or extroverted you are, no matter what your skill set, how many people you interact with, your physical condition—God wants to work through you exactly as you are. He made you the way you are to serve a purpose. His purpose.

We are like a garden of wildflowers. Each is unique, each is special and each is deliberately created by God for a unique purpose. Each is dependent upon the other and God to fulfill their purpose.

Relax. It's not about you, your strengths or weaknesses. To surrender yourself to Him is the beginning of purpose. It is His work and he has merely invited you along for the ride.

When we experience worry or fear about the future is when we are betting on our own skills rather than God's. If we trust that His strength is enough, that He is constantly available to us, that He loves us more than we can imagine and wants to help us, then there is no fear, no worry. He will carry us through. Trust that God loves you. Trust that He is working through you and see what happens.

"However, as it is written:
'No eye has seen, no ear has heard, no mind has conceived what God has prepared for those who love him'—but God has revealed it to us by his Spirit." 1 Corinthians 2: 9-10

CHAPTER 5: IT'S ALL ABOUT YOU

"For he chose us in him before the creation of the world to be holy and blameless in his sight. In love." Ephesians 1:4

"But we ought always to thank God for you, brothers loved by the Lord, because from the beginning God chose you to be saved through the sanctifying work of the Spirit and through belief in the truth." 2 Thessalonians 2:13

This whole thing is about you. Before the creation, before time, God knew you and loved you. He loves you now and He will never leave you. You are the apple of his eye, created in His image and destined for eternal, joyful, peaceful, loving relationship with Him.

Here is a mystery. When He thinks of you He thinks only of you. He is fully present with you and loving toward you. Your concerns, fears and joys are His as well. There are no secrets. He knows the whole you and He loves you. You may ask, "Well, then what about everyone else?" The mystery is that He is the same with every person. How does He do that? I don't know. It's a mystery.

You are the reason He willingly paid the ultimate price to make a way for you to live with Him forever. The only remaining obstacle you face is your own choice. He will not force himself upon you. You must choose freely to love Him. That's how much God loves you. How much do you love yourself?

"Love the Lord your God with all your heart, with all your soul, and with all your mind. Love your neighbor as yourself."

Think about that second commandment for a moment: He said, love your neighbor AS YOURSELF. Why would he put it like that? He could have just left it at "Love your neighbor" or "Love your neighbor as I love you" but he didn't. It's almost as if he sneaked a third commandment in there: Love yourself.

Learn to be okay with yourself. This is another tall order that is only attained one moment at a time. If you're going to know yourself it will be through Him. If you are going to know others it will be through Him. If you are going to be known by others it will be through Him. God made us to be in relationship, and relationship is a two-way thing; we need to be known as well as to know. ALL of it happens through Him.

God doesn't make mistakes. There is a reason that the first commandment is to Love the Lord completely; the more you hang out with God, the more you will sense His unconditional love for you and that changes how you feel about yourself.

"There is no condemnation in Christ Jesus." (Romans 8:1)

You get love, hope, peace but no judgments. All the negative thoughts are coming from some source other than God. If you are going to change it will be because you love and are being loved. You can't truly love your neighbor unless you love yourself. You can look good, but you're never going to experience the fullness of a relationship with another person if you don't have a relationship with God that teaches you to love yourself.

When we think about some of the things we tell ourselves, it can be pretty appalling. "I'm so stupid." "I'll never be good enough." "I'm so fat it's disgusting." We say things to ourselves that we would never dream of saying to another person and that God, our heavenly loving Father, would never, ever say to us. Imagine how you would feel if you heard your son tell your daughter that she was stupid. That's probably how God feels when we say those things to ourselves. How could we criticize His perfect creation so easily?

Before the beginning of time He knew you and He loved you. In the womb He knew you and he loved you. Today He knows you and loves you. He will never leave you or forsake you. When creation began and ever since. He desires an ongoing and growing relationship with you.

One of the reasons for our negative and derogatory thoughts are that we often compare ourselves to others. There will always be people who are better, smarter, stronger, thinner, taller, shorter and so on. God does not compare us to one another. When He looks at you he sees the person He beautifully and deliberately created. He knows completely who you are today. And He loves you.

Your life here is all about His love for you, His hopes for you, His desire to have an intimate relationship with you. He knows you and loves you and wants you to know and be known to others through His love. God is not limited by space and time like we are so He is always with you and completely present. We can't be fully present all the time with everyone but, when we practice being present as much as possible, we are following God's lead. Whether or not to practice is up to us.

He created you with the ability to choose. He will not impose himself on you. He has already chosen you. You must choose him. An authentic relationship involves two parties and cannot be forced.

"Come now, let us reason together," says the LORD. "Though your sins are like scarlet, they shall be as white as snow; though they are red as crimson, they shall be like wool." Isaiah 1:18

CHAPTER 6: SUMMARY OF PART 1

1. Jesus told us our purpose quite clearly in the Bible:

"And one of them, an expert in religious law, asked him a question to test him: 'Teacher, which commandment in the law is the greatest?' Jesus said to him, 'Love the Lord your God with all your heart, with all your soul, and with all your mind.' This is the first and greatest commandment. The second is like it: 'Love your neighbor as yourself.' All the law and the prophets depend on these two commandments." Matthew 22:35-40

2. Authentic relationships are built one interaction at a time.

3. There is no such thing as a "random interaction".

4. You cannot accomplish this alone. You are fully dependent on God and others.

5. Before time, God created you for authentic relationship.

PART 2-RELATIONSHIP APPLIED

Writing a book on authentic relationship requires writing the book *in* authentic relationship. The next section of the book is a collection of essays written by friends. Each chapter is a reflection of his or her personal experience with relationship: with their families, in the workplace, in the church, and with boundaries and addiction. Their stories illustrate that relationships are most often messy, hard work and broadly diverse. Were it not for the unspeakable beauty of the peace, fulfillment and irreplaceable meaning that relationship provides, it would not be worth the effort.

The authorship of these chapters is a demonstration of the points God wants to express through us.

We are not meant to do this alone.

CHAPTER 7:
THE POWER OF RELATIONSHIP

BY JOHN BATEMAN

I was a little surprised when my dear friend, Paul Evanson, asked me to contribute a chapter to this book on relationship. As you will see in the following paragraphs, I am certainly not an expert on the topic. But what I've slowly discovered is that it was not how good or bad I was at relationships; it was finally recognizing the significant role they play in how we function through life. Writing this has been an amazing experience for which I'm thankful. Here is my story.

The Preacher's son

Almost 30 years ago, my father committed suicide. Having my father take his own life was shocking, but it was even more unbelievable because he'd been a Baptist Preacher for most of his adult life. My father's death shook not only the core of our family, but also the many believers that had been involved in and outside of his ministry. He had not only preached locally, but had also participated in ministries and preached abroad, particularly in the Asian countries. He smuggled films into America showing the hate crimes of Red China against believers. He helped sneak New Testament bibles disguised as Mao's red handbook into Red China so that believers could have the written word without reprisal. He was also in "Who's Who in America" 1975-76 for his endeavors in Korea and Taiwan. How could this man who preached the hope and love of God, fall into such despair and take his life? He left my mom, my sister, and my three brothers and me confused and lost. Worst of all, he deprived us of the opportunity to have closure or heal over the strange family dynamics that ultimately led each of us into destructive lifestyles.

Outwardly he appeared a mighty man of God, but inwardly; he was a man in crisis. I can remember from early in my childhood waking up many nights from the sound of my father sobbing. The man that smiled for cameras and encouraged large audiences of believers didn't live at my house. My father cared about the *things* of God, the *image* of Christianity and the "law," but seemingly cared little about an authentic relationship with God or his family. At home, the law was the focus. We were expected to be exemplary, and the punishment was severe when we misbehaved; he saw our misbehavior as a personal insult to him. It was a hard regime to live under. I remember standing at the stop of the stairs, screaming "Why can't we just be normal without God!" then I ripped a bible into pieces and threw it down the stairs. (My father was in Taiwan at the time, so I live to tell you this story.)

Regardless of the fear I felt around my father, I still longed to have a relationship with him. I remember one time when I was about ten years old, I overheard some boys at school talking about their dads taking them fishing. It prompted me to ask my dad if he would take me fishing. He said yes, and even promised to take me on the weekend. I was excited all week about that fishing trip; in fact, I hardly thought of anything else. Over and over, I pictured us together, on the lake, poles in hand—the Norman Rockwell version of a father/son fishing trip.

The weekend arrived. I found my father and asked what time we would be leaving. He looked at me questioningly and said, "Leaving where?" I said matter of factly, "Fishing. We are going fishing today, remember?" I could tell he had been caught off guard, but rather than be apologetic, he actually raised his voice and in a tone of exasperation said, "We can't go fishing son, I have to take the servicemen shopping."

Relationship

Some Korean servicemen were in town, and I later learned that they had gone shopping for televisions. Ironically, my father was so repulsed by what was on TV that we were not allowed to have a TV in our home and were instructed not to watch it anywhere. Breaking his promise to me was bad enough, but when I found out why, the pain turned to anger and I couldn't bear his hypocrisy. I have never forgotten that day. I can still feel the emotions I had—humiliation, rejection, and on top of it, I had actually been scolded. We didn't go fishing then—or ever. Looking back, I suppose this event marked the beginning of my rebellion.

By the time I hit my teenage years, my anger had begun to define me. The tender, sensitive boy I had been began to look like a weak child to me, so I got tough. Creating an image of a "bad" boy finally helped me fit in with my peers—and fitting in was my priority. At sixteen, I had run away from home four times and had been in juvenile hall twice. My father picked me up after the last incarceration and let me know what a loser I was. He berated me and said that I was destined for prison and had no purpose or value. As he raged on, I remember his voice felt like a sledge hammer pounding at my soul, destroying who I was, and leaving who I was meant to be beneath the rubble. I hated my father and wished that he would die. As horrible as it sounds, my hate was like a suit of armor that protected my heart and devalued any power he once had in my life.

Amazingly, I survived my teen years. Then, as a young adult, I found my way back to the church and gave my life to the Lord. It was an amazing transformation. I felt free from the past, filled with new hope and peace. I also began to play music in the church and for the first time recognized my own calling. I felt motivated to share my experience with my father and began to call and write to establish some relational connection.

I visited my parents in San Diego, but I could see that his heart wasn't really into the visit. He was apparently depressed over the fact that my sister, Debbie, the apple of his eye, had married an Hispanic man. I tried to encourage him to put his hope and trust in Jesus, but he said, "That doesn't work for me." Here I stood before him, saved, doing the right thing and I could see it made no difference. The fact that he was lamenting over my sister's marriage sent me over the edge.

I began to tell him how he had made me feel growing up. I brought up the many times I had tried to reach out to him and was rejected. I asked him "Why didn't you love me?" He took his glasses off and said "Go ahead and hit me; I won't resist you." I felt foolish and walked away that day vowing to never make myself vulnerable with him again.

The vow was short lived, however and within a few months I wrote him a letter in which I shared how sorry I was for being disrespectful. I asked him to forgive me for not being the son I should have been to him. A week went by and I didn't hear from him. I was anxious and hoped my letter would be yet another olive branch that would be received with joy and that we would have the father/son relationship my heart still longed for. It was a Tuesday morning when my grandmother called to tell me that my father had taken his life. He never read my letter.

My father was gone. I was devastated, knowing that the approval and love I longed for was outside the realm of possibility. What I had needed from my father that day I confronted him was to embrace me and tell me he was sorry for his rejection, but instead he made himself a martyr. Now, there would never be an embrace, an apology, nor would we reconcile and have the relationship I needed so desperately. This became my new "story"—I became a victim and his death changed the course of my life.

Like father, like son.

Relationship

I was married and had my daughter at the time of his death, but traveled to San Diego to attend the funeral alone. After returning home I began to change. I was angry at God. I felt that He let me down and found it hard to have a relationship with the "Father" when my experience with my own father had destroyed me in so many ways.

The only place I felt love and safety during that time, was when I was with my daughter, and just like my father's daughter was to him, she was the apple of my eye. I was good to her, loving her, caring for her and found myself to be a doting father. This was not the case for the other child in my life. My wife had a son from a previous marriage that I tolerated, but inwardly felt resentful of. I treated him poorly enough that eventually his father intervened and my stepson left our home for a year and a half.

My wife was broken hearted and could not be consoled. I knew she felt torn between her son and now a husband and stepdaughter. I'm sure she felt trapped and merely existed through that horrible time. Every visit from her young son would mean so much, but each time he left, she would retreat in pain. Once my wife's son returned to our home permanently, he and I did have a better relationship. I treated him well and we grew closer over time. The damage in my marriage, however, was done; my wife distanced herself from me for obvious reasons. Regardless of my efforts to be a better stepfather, I was unable to sincerely hold myself responsible for their separation. Instead, I began to resent my wife for her treatment of me, blaming her for our marital issues.

It's strange to think back on it—how could I not see that I had become so much like my father? How could I have not cared that I was hurting this little boy? As I look back, I am astonished that I was capable of such cruelty to an innocent child. Ultimately, my marriage began to crumble along with my faith. Rather than turn toward God, I ran in a different direction.

I joined a band, and started playing music in clubs, and at weddings and other venues. I also joined a gym and worked out very hard, eventually changing the way I looked physically. Between attention from women, compliments on my music and being promoted to supervisor at work, I had reinvented myself. For the first time, my life finally seemed full. Working a day job and playing at night, eventually led to drug use, but only enough to function. Somewhere along the way, I had quit caring: about God, about my wife, about our marriage. I had turned a corner in my life and had no interest in going back.

In 1987, a couple of friends and I started a new band and landed a job as the house band in a popular club. That's where I met Toni. She was a free spirit; she loved to have fun, was engaging, and had a confidence and qualities I had never seen before. More importantly, she made me feel special, valued, desired and important in a way no one else ever had. We became friends and soon afterward, I moved out of our family home.

Toni and I became intimate which was a huge conflict for me. I hid our relationship and she could not understand why or what would make me feel so guilty. She didn't understand the whole "Christian" thing and had never heard the gospel. One night, I shared the story of Jesus with her. Right there, in a dark time of my life, having an affair, I told her about His love for mankind, how He was treated, and how He ultimately hung on a cross as a sacrifice for us. She was in tears by the time I finished—she didn't know how to respond to this feeling at that point, but later realized that night was a prelude to understanding her need for a relationship with Jesus.

My ex-wife moved to another town after the divorce. Wanting a new beginning myself, I left my job, my band and the people I knew and moved to another town, about three hours away. I also left Toni. By this time, I knew I should not be with a woman that had three sons. I wanted to be single for a while; I didn't think it was appropriate to just jump right into another committed relationship. But that didn't last long. Toni and I had a very difficult time being apart, and by the time I left the town we'd been living in, I had already fallen in love with her. When she came to visit me one summer, we agreed to move in together. It was just her, my daughter, Jenny, and I, so things were wonderful. When Toni's sons joined us that fall, I began treating them with the same resentment I'd had toward my first wife's son, but this time I was a little sneakier about it.

God is amazing and continued reaching out to Toni through a woman in the new neighborhood and Toni surrendered her life to Christ. Remarkably, it was the following week when Toni confronted me for the first time about my treatment of her youngest son. She said she would leave me and that I needed to make some choices before our relationship went any further. That night, I wrote a letter to God and rededicated my life to Christ. I began attending church again. Toni and I got married as an act of obedience and started this new journey together, praying and seeking God's will for our lives. We began to play in the worship team and became leaders in the church. Worshipping God through music has always been the easiest avenue to express myself. Regardless of my heart's condition at any given time, when I sing to the Lord I feel connected. Whether creating a worship set list, practicing songs or leading the congregation, I could sense God's presence in my life and felt confident in His love for me.

Home was a different story. Much like my father, my church family saw one man, but my wife and kids experienced someone different at home. I continued to be harsh with the boys, favoring my daughter and rationalizing my behavior. I knew in my heart it was wrong and would try harder. There would be times when things would get better, when I could maintain control, but underneath, I still resented my stepsons. In hindsight, I can see that they experienced the same rejection and legalism I had loathed as a child. Rather than admit I was the problem, I continued to rely on my "victim" persona. How could I be a good father since I was never shown what a father should be? I refused to take responsibility for my behavior.

Over the next several years, I was off and on leading worship. I would get frustrated with the musicality of the worship team, the pastor, the pressure, the diversity and rather than focus on individual relationships or try to work through it, I would quit. The behavior toward my stepsons continued and my wife became increasingly frustrated. She challenged me continually, pleading with me that if I couldn't love her boys, to at least show them the same consideration that I showed my daughter, but I couldn't. The tension over my relationship (or lack of relationship) with my stepsons continued to be the governing force in my relationship with my wife.

Just when you thought it couldn't get worse.

The emptiness inside me grew, and I found myself resenting Toni for not relieving my pain the way she once did. I again blamed the kids for taking her attention from me, and started to justify my feelings. I actually didn't know if I loved Toni any longer. There was a female co-worker who gave me the attention I so desperately thought I needed. The more things that went wrong at home, the closer I got with the other woman (who was also married). When Toni learned that I was questioning my feelings for her, she said she would never be with someone that didn't love her and she would leave. That weekend, Toni went to her grandmother's house and my female co-worker showed up to comfort me. I fell into temptation—she and I slept together. After this encounter; we both felt awkward, but kept up the pleasantries, until she left. After she had gone, I fell on the floor, barely able to breath. "God please forgive me!" I cried, "What have I done? I love my wife!"

Toni learned of the betrayal and confronted me at work. Over the next few weeks, I became increasingly broken. The fear of what would happen, my betrayal of the woman I loved and my children overwhelmed me. I was falling deeper and deeper into despair. One day at a customer's house, the pain was so horrible I called a Christian co-worker and asked him to help me. When he arrived at the customer's home, I was kneeling on the garage floor sobbing. I had nothing left in me that could reconcile this pain. This man began to walk through my pain with me for several months. He prayed and encouraged me to place all of my hope in God. He continually reminded me of the grace and forgiveness that was waiting for me as soon as I could accept it. This was my first relational experience with a believer. He didn't try to fix me or tell me what I should do—he simply walked through the experience with me. He would often say that our hopeless life could only be secure in knowing the Lord. (Many years later I would understand what "<u>knowing</u>" the Lord meant).

Through this relationship, and my wife's grace and love, my marriage did not end. Although she suffered tremendously through the shame and pain I had caused her and my family, the love God placed in my wife was greater than the sin that I had chosen. I knew I had to take responsibility for my unfaithfulness. All of my co-workers knew what I had done. There were times I overheard them talk about me, "The man of God who committed adultery." I was the all-knowing manager, once admired, now scorned. I knew in my heart that this was a consequence and set my course on walking through this by putting my trust in God.

One day, the woman I had been intimate with told me that Toni had called her and asked her to lunch. She was terrified, but I encouraged her to go. Toni had been working on the youth skit for the Easter service, when the Lord impressed on her that she needed to forgive this woman. Toni shared God's love and forgave the woman. Then, to the woman's surprise, Toni asked *her* for forgiveness. She explained, "I was once the adulteress."

I wish I could say that this was the turning point in my life, but there were still bridges that I had to cross. As the years went on, I would feel like I was "there" only to slip back to old patterns the minute the struggle with church, family or work distracted me. Even after the kids grew up and married, I still hindered Toni's relationship with her boys and family. After everything I'd gone through, I still moved further and further away from relationships, complaining that my wife was over involved with her family and friends. To avoid family showing up, I would tell her I needed "down" time and wasted away in front of the TV in the garage. By this time she had begun to travel and was gone over 50% of the time. One day she said, "You are alone all the time, how much downtime do you need?" In a moment of truth I told her there would never be enough and I began counseling.

I could tell that Toni was beginning to pull away. She had endured my endless cycles of good and bad behavior and finally decided that if things didn't change, she had had enough. She would give our marriage just one more chance. She suggested marriage counseling, but told me if things didn't change as a result, our marriage was over.

At my first session alone with the counselor, I began to tell her that our problems were a result of my wife's over involvement with her children and I had even checked her phone to see how many times she spoke with them. When my wife had her counseling session, she was quizzed on how much time she spent with her children and quickly realized this would go nowhere unless the truth of my own issues was exposed.

She came home angry and hurt. In all we had been through, I had never seen her like that. Despite seeing her pain, and knowing that this was my last opportunity to save our marriage, I launched into my self-defense. I told her that her kids were dependent, that they couldn't do anything without her. I even threw in scripture "a man shall leave his father and mother and cling to his wife." But she knew the truth about her relationship with her children. They were independent, hard working, devoted husbands and fathers and good men. She was fully confident in the fact that she had a healthy, close relationship with not only her sons, but her entire family. She was done with my accusations.

Relationship

My wife was not raised in a godly home. Her father was abusive—physically, sexually and emotionally. He was also abusive to her mother. Sometimes their fights would wake the children and they would see their mother bloody and bruised. Every so often, her mother would try to leave. Toni and her younger brother and sister were forced to take only what could fit into a garbage sack and leave everything behind, only to find themselves back with their father within a couple of months. The vicious cycle went on throughout their childhood yet somehow, these children knew how to love and grew close to one another. They didn't remain victims and although they certainly have had emotional struggles along the way, they found strength in relationships and knew the importance of family. They are also loyal to a fault. It is very hard for them to give up on anyone and my wife had finally seen that no matter what she did or said, or even how much she loved me, she was incapable of changing me. She recognized the same cycles she had experienced as a child and knew it was time to go.

That night, she said, "I think you should be alone. I have loved your daughter and have never stood in the way of you being the parent you wanted to be to her. I have honored and supported your close relationship with her son. I've supported you and your family even when they rejected me. Yet, no matter what I do, you cannot reciprocate. I have not been free to be the mother or grandmother I should have been to my sons and grandchildren. I do not want to live the rest of my life defending my love for my family. I will not go through another generation of this." She went on to say, "You say you love me, but your actions say something entirely different. If you did love me, you would value and respect the only thing of real importance to me and that is relationships." I started to respond, but she asked me, "Isn't God about relationships?"

I didn't know how to respond, in fact, I said, "I've got nowhere to go." All she wanted from me was respect and love. She also wanted me to have relationships with those she loved and she reminded me that despite their childhood, her sons had stood beside me and loved me. I knew, there was no more hiding. For the first time in my life, I was determined to change. I looked into her eyes—filled with pain, disappointment and grief—and my heart broke for her. God *is* about relationship. I promised her: "I will honestly do the work to see why I continue to behave like this."

Relationship "101"

When I was finally able to see the hurt I was causing my wife, who was also my best friend, I realized I was in trouble and began to draw near to God for the answer. A friend of mine gave me a copy of "The Shack." Although there are varying opinions over the story, nothing I'd read in my past so clearly painted a picture of God like that. I found myself viewing not only a savior, but a friend. An approachable, compassionate Father. I began to view the Lord in a different light.It was amazing that after all the years of studying Greek and Hebrew, working my way through the history of Christianity, trying to understand God—I had missed the most important thing of all; The Lord wanted a relationship with me. For the first time in my life, I began to understand that God loved me. I even bought the audio version of The Shack and listened to it over and over. Something was still missing, though. I knew I was loved, but how did that translate to loving others and how could someone, other than God, really love me?

Relationships have always been a challenge to me. Other than the friend that walked through my pain with me so long ago, I was uncomfortable with authenticity and was very controlled in what I presented to people in my life. Some people saw through that, but when they pushed to get in, I would back away or feel overwhelmed and would let the relationship fade. Occasionally, my wife would bring it to my attention. One time she said, "I'm your only friend, so when I'm mad at you, you are friendless." In truth, my worth was based on what type of feedback I got from people around me. People that complimented me or knew me as an acquaintance fed my sense of self-worth. I would share enough to appear authentic, but if there was even a hint of judgment, I ended the relationship.

I started to attend a local church and ran into an acquaintance from previous years—Paul, the author of this book. He told me that I'd been on his mind lately. We just laughed it off and went our way. The next Sunday I saw Paul again, and he said "You are still on my mind a lot; we should get together and talk." We set up a meeting and began to share our stories. The first conversation was acknowledging that neither one of us knew how to be a friend. During the first several meetings I was more concerned with how I would be perceived and struggled with being completely honest, but over the course of time becoming transparent became natural. Our relationship evolved into an authentic friendship. As trust grew, honesty came more easily. The Lord gave me strength to share my brokenness, my vulnerabilities and my needs. The desire to continue hiding was losing its ground. That first meeting was three and a half years ago, and we still continue our weekly meetings. We have no agenda, we just talk and the Lord always shows up. There is no "fixing" or "judging"—just trusting that God will guide the way. Forming a friendship with Paul and sharing our stories has been an anchor for me.

As we continue our walk together, God is showing me the blessings of being in relationship with Him and with others, like Paul and my wife. It doesn't mean that things are easy—life still has its challenges. One of those challenges is the depression and anxiety I've struggled with for most of my life. For the most part, I could handle it, but not too long ago these episodes became crippling, impacting my sleep and my job. I was terrified, but unable to understand why. As the anxiety continued, I felt out of control and was very sensitive to the fact that my wife didn't need one more burden at this time. Between supporting several family members through difficult divorces and dealing with the loss of her mom, Toni's plate was more than full. But I had no one to turn to; she was the only friend I had ever depended on. My hope began to shrivel and once again. I felt like a scared, desperate child and had no idea why. I instantly felt distant from God, and once again the feelings of not measuring up took hold of me and bound me with chains of fear. I even began to question God's love for me again.

Somehow, I continued to meet each week with Paul throughout this time. There was no hiding my condition from him and he insisted that I see a doctor. He accompanied me to the appointment and advocated for me to get medication to help calm me and get some sleep. He also introduced me to a Christian counselor, who later became another person that helped me through this painful time in my life. Paul came to the rescue, showing up with grace and heartfelt concern. I had never experienced this before and I am so thankful he was there.

The counselor he recommended was unlike any counselor I'd had before. She really did care. She was full of grace, compassion and seemed to "get" me, but was also able to help me move though the painful childhood experiences that kept showing up each time I felt any sort of rejection or challenge. She also provided me with coping skills to use whenever I faced challenges and those hurtful childhood moments threatened to derail me. I began to see once again—God was showing up. He was my only answer and when I could not seem to sense His presence, He would appear and love me through his children, my friends, my caregivers—through relationship. I found myself thankful that God had placed this counselor in my life.

My wife has also been thankful. She has seen the biggest change in my walk (even though I still trip over my feet) since having a "true" friend. She also learned to trust that it was time for healing and she no longer intervenes for me with the boys. I was finally on the right track and I guess God thought I was finally ready for one of the most emotional moments of my life. Little did I know that the "one chance" with one of my stepsons, was just around the corner.

Rest in peace

Relationship

By now, it should be clear to anyone reading this story that my relationship with my father on Earth has interfered with every relationship in my life, including the one with my Father in heaven. Over the past year, I finally feel like I have been able to face this truth myself and allow the Holy Spirit to take what I knew in my head and let it influence my heart.

I am certainly not the only one who was impacted by my father. All of his children have similar stories. Drug abuse, destroyed marriages, unhealthy behaviors, extreme relationships with God and church—each of my siblings' stories could fill the pages of a book. Sadly, there are many of the grandchildren that have paid a price as well. To this day, it is rare during any family time that my father isn't brought into the conversation. Some of us hate him, some pity him, some of us long for what never was and never can be. My mother is 87 and to this day, still grieves over the loss of her husband. She is the only one of us that remained faithful to God, trusting her precious Lord every step of the way. For years, she has prayed and cried out to Him for comfort. The "why" of his suicide still haunts her and watching her children struggle has kept my father's life a focal point for our family—especially my mom. He is often the scapegoat, "If only your father would have..." How do you let go of someone that has so clearly defined your life? Why have I allowed him to live on in me instead of refusing to put a stop to the abuse? When does it stop?

In order for damaged relationships to heal from abuse, the abuser must take responsibility for his behavior. Often, like with my dad, that opportunity never arises. Lucky for me, I did get that opportunity—not as the victim, but as the abuser. Some time ago, I was confronted by my middle stepson, Brady. It was an intense conversation and at one point, he asked me why I was so distant from him when he was a child. He now has two sons and couldn't imagine ever treating them the way he was treated by me. At first I retreated and responded with the usual line I'd used in the past, "Well, I didn't have a great childhood and never learned how to be a father...". It didn't work that day; Brady demanded the truth.

I did not want to answer. I knew the truth in my heart but it was daunting to say it out loud. But I knew, this was MY father moment…was I going to take off my glasses and tell him to go ahead and hit me? No. The time had come for honesty. I knew that he was giving me an opportunity to be truthful and heal our relationship—an opportunity that might never come again.

Taking a deep breath, I confessed to him: "Because…I didn't love you."

After a long silence, he said he understood.

This was the first time I had been honest about my behavior toward my sons. I had never been here before. It was frightening, but the person in front of me was worth the unknown result of my truthfulness. Our relationship began from this moment. In that moment, my mindset completely shifted from thinking of him as someone I "had to" have a relationship with, to someone I *wanted* to have a relationship with.

I have to say, though, that it never occurred to me until I began to write this story, how it must have felt for him to hear those words. I decided to ask him. This is what he wrote:

John called me today with a question that gave me some pause. It was something I guess I hadn't ever really reflected back on, which becomes important a little later on. John wanted to talk about an incident that happened between the two of us a few years ago.

I went through a pretty severe bout of anger back in 2008 following my separation from the Navy. A lot of the frustrations of life were coming to a head and this opened up the floodgates for many things I had not yet dealt with. One of those was my relationship with John. I hated what he had done to me, or maybe even more, what he hadn't done for me. Knowing that I had gained his respect and that his heart had

Relationship

grown tender with age, did not heal the feelings of inadequacy I'd carried all of those years.

I had expressed my anger to mom during a time that John was really just coming to the realization that he was truly dysfunctional with his "relationships" and was beginning an entirely new process; self-awareness in lieu of self-wallowing. I think that of all the perspective changes that John promised or claimed over the years, this was the first time mom believed it was real in her heart. She had pressured me to talk to him rather than continue to live frustrated with the lack of authenticity in our relationship. I think her true fear was that rejection from me may cause John to plummet back into the abyss, like a newly clean drug addict...at least that's what I thought. After about a year of contemplation I started to soften. My pride began to weaken and the need for closure seeped in through the cracks.

I finally got the courage to confront John. We had gone to my niece's birthday party and I asked John to ride home with me so I could talk to him. It didn't go well. In fact it nearly became disastrous. But he began to compromise. He allowed me just a few comments at a time and then he would make an irrational comment. The things he said were clearly born of self-preservation and an instinct to make it someone else's issue but he would compromise a little more each time. In about two hours John and I were talking for the first time in my life.

So, like I said, John called me today to ask me about my feelings about that conversation. The day that John and I had this talk, there were some very profound moments—especially the part where he told me that he hadn't loved me as a child. Don't get me wrong, he tried NOT to say it but it's always been there, like a ghost at our table, lingering far too long.

What John wanted to know today was how that made me feel to hear that from him. I felt validated. For the first time in my life I felt that my pain as a child was valid. I'd grown up being called too sensitive or a big baby, but I wasn't that at all; I was insightful to a fault. See, I knew John loved adult Brady but I also knew that what I had felt back then was real to me. What I never could have predicted though was how badly I needed it to be real to him.

It's this simple; it would not have ever been possible for John and I to have an organic and true relationship as adults had I continued to live believing that the past held two very different stories for each of us regarding our relationship. So oddly enough; the fallout of all of this is trust. That day was the beginning of trust between John and I.

So, this is the part that John DIDN'T ask me to write down. I mentioned earlier that his question regarding my feelings when he admitted that he didn't love me, gave me pause. The significance of this whole thing is, I hadn't thought about it. Looking back, I realize now why I was so angry.

It wasn't about the love, which was sad. It was the fact that I was held hostage by these feelings. Regardless of all my personal growth, my time in the Navy, being a good Dad and a loving husband...nothing I could achieve would lift me above the need for closure with this man whom I needed desperately to trust. I'd worked so hard to recover from my shame and to heal my self-image but to do so, I needed to put a check in every box.

The result of the truth was trust and love. I truly forgave John for those years, to the point of forgetting the statement all together until he asked me about it. That is healing.

Brady's words to me, the forgiveness and healing that he, my wife Toni, and many others have granted me, have changed me forever. Though it's not always easy, God is opening my heart to authentic relationships with Him and others. He has taken what was broken and made it new. I may never have closure with my father, but I now see that *I* can provide closure to those that have been victimized by *my* behavior. I have seen that the truth can set you (and others) free. I can be loved, I can love, and I can have friends and be a friend. I can have peace and joy, not because I'm surrounded with admirers, but because I am loved by God. I may be my father's son, but I'm also my Father's son and can no longer live my life crippled by a past I had no control over. I need to trust that God can close the void and provide me the comfort and security I have always wanted.

Dear Dad,

Rest in peace

Love, John

Dear friends, let us love one another, for love comes from God. Everyone who loves has been born of God and <u>knows</u> God. **John 4:7**

CHAPTER 8:
RELATIONSHIP WITHIN BOUNDARIES:
JUST SAY NO TO CARPOOLING

BY DANA KELLER

The carpool wasn't working. My sophomore son's high school is a half an hour from our house, so when I was approached during the summer by the mother of a freshman girl looking to work out a carpool, it seemed like a great idea. *I'd take five hours in the car per week instead of ten any day!* I thought. There was only one problem: We are not carpool people.

My 15-year-old knew it. When he groused and complained, I told him he was being selfish. It was *my* time and *my* gas money, so he was doing it for *me*, I explained. He could put up with two freshmen girls for an hour a day. I mean, how bad could it be? We arranged the first week, with me generally driving in the afternoons, and the other mom generally driving in the mornings. A third mom had contacted us and she would not be driving; her daughter only needed a ride home a few afternoons a week, so she just paid us per trip. Perfect.

The first few weeks were tolerable. The schedule seemed to work out pretty well, save for a few schedule changes here and there. The ride was almost intolerably awkward, with no conversation whatsoever, but that would change, I reasoned, as the kids got to know each other. It was nice, after all, to spend less time in the car…even though I was driving an extra fifteen minutes every time I drove since the girls lived a little east of us and I was providing door-to-door service.

It seemed with each week that there were more and more changes and the arrangement was becoming increasingly complex. I found myself not being able to schedule anything because I wasn't sure when I was driving, or I'd plan something only to have to move it because it didn't work with the other mom's schedule. The car trips, if anything, got *more* awkward. To top it off, even though I was the one driving the "pay per trip" girl, the other mom wanted to split the money with me. Each week, I found myself more and more stressed by the entire situation.

My son had only one thing to say: "I told you so." And he smiled as he said it. Schmuck.

He did tell me so. He knew what I should have known all along: We are not carpool people. Now, something had to be done about it, and *I* had to do it because it was *my* stress and *my* inconvenience that was making this unworkable. Crap. I had to be a real grown-up. With boundaries.

I don't have a lot of experience with boundaries, despite my 44 years on this planet. For a variety of reasons, familial and cultural, I am not good at saying no, or for standing up for myself when something isn't working for me. The world I was raised in taught that kids didn't get to have a say in things, that girls should be "nice"…and nice meant putting others' feelings before our own. Saying "no, this doesn't work for me" was *not* being nice.

What I didn't realize at the time, though, was that authentic relationships *require* boundaries. I wasn't really in relationship with all those people I thought I was pleasing—or trying to please—because I wasn't being honest with them about what I really thought or felt. Real relationships are strong enough to take negative emotions and honest discussion. If the people whose expectations I was trying to live up to *knew* I felt resentful or overwhelmed or angry, would they really want my participation?

I carried this philosophy of "just say yes" with me through most of my life. I said yes indiscriminately because saying "no" wasn't an option in my mind. If I didn't have time for something, I made time for it—regardless of what kind of toll it took on my family or me. Eventually, my life was living me rather than the other way around. Much like the carpool, our lives weren't working. *My* life wasn't working. All those years of acquiescing behavior crescendoed into one, giant psychological and emotional crash.

I couldn't figure out why I felt so unhappy: I had a great marriage, wonderful (if not challenging) sons, a small bevvy of friends, and work that I was good at. It didn't make sense to me. I couldn't see that what I had built was a house of cards, without a firm foundation, because—with the exception of my husband and kids—the relationships I'd built were not based on authenticity. They had no depth or intimacy, leaving a giant hole in my heart that needed filling, despite my busy schedule and multiple connections.

I found a great life coach/counselor and slowly began the work of learning about *boundaries*. Boundaries are the wonderful little fences around our bountiful gardens of life. They have gates, so we can invite people in to share our abundant gifts—people can pick flowers or baskets of fruit. And sometimes, we can shut those gates, so we can tend to the garden, water it, carefully prune, and take away the weeds so we can continue to have gifts to share. Without these fences, our gardens eventually become bare, trodden, and so overrun with weeds, it can be hard to tell where the fruit-bearing plants once were.

The idea that our time and talents are a treasure to be guarded and shared in a purposeful way was new to me. To me, it wasn't nice to tell someone they couldn't have something of mine—an hour here or there, a ride for their kid, or cookies for

Relationship

the school open house. *Nice women, good moms, don't say no.* But look where that kind of thinking got me. Something had to change.

Initially (after "the crash"), I said no to everything. I was physically and emotionally exhausted so it was easy to say no. I quit taking on clients in my consulting business. I stopped volunteering at school. I completely cleared my schedule. It was fantastic for a while. *So this is what boundaries are like!*, I thought, but I was wrong.

We can't live a life of just no, no, no, either. I finally built the fence, but if no one can share the bounty of my garden, what good is it? Humans, by our very nature, are meant to be in relationship, and we can't do that if we're not sharing our gifts. My fence, it seemed, needed a gate.

Slowly I began to carefully consider opportunities as they came my way. With much reflection and discussion with my husband and friends, I began to discern which things I wanted to say yes to. Writing group?: Yes. Project for health care company?: No. And then, eventually…Carpooling?: Yes.

The thing about establishing boundaries is that there is more to it than just building the fence and the gate, and choosing who and what you invite in. Sometimes you invite someone in and eventually you find that they're taking too many apples, or they trampled your hydrangeas. How, then, do you politely ask someone to leave? Nice people can't possibly do that!

With this weekend's flurry of carpool e-mails, I knew it was time; I had to ask my carpool cohorts to leave the garden. I agonized over the phone calls. My years of previous experience in these types of situations almost always resulted in me giving in to some kind of compromise that still didn't work for me because I just couldn't reconcile saying no with being nice. This time it had to be different and I wasn't sure I was up to the task.

Thank God (literally) for dear friends because a quick call to my friend Maureen helped me solidify my stance. This isn't working for me. Period. No need to explain or justify. I could just say no in a kind, respectful way and leave it at that. No one was wrong, it just didn't work.

Of course, the phone calls went much better than I expected. While my partners in carpooling did try to talk me into some alternatives, I just left it at "no." It felt good to show up to that conversation as a nice person who could also confidently stand up for myself and what I needed. While the whole situation caused a lot of angst, it was good practice for what I'm sure will be more to come.

I had no idea how nice it would feel to see my garden overflowing with gorgeous flowers and luscious fruit. I'm glad I took the time to tend it. The fence protects it just enough, and the gate needs a little oil to the hinges now and then, but it works just fine. So come on in! Pick a bouquet, enjoy some raspberries, and just know that sometimes, I might have to ask you to leave. And that doesn't make me "not nice." It makes me a healthy, happy adult that values and cultivates her time and talents in order to create authentic relationships with the people in my life. And I'm okay with that.

CHAPTER 9: RELATIONSHIP IN THE WORKPLACE: LESSONS IN LEADERSHIP FROM THE MILITARY

BY MARK AMMONS

My Early Experience

On a Friday night after I completed the field medical course for corpsmen (medics in the Navy), I reported to my new unit. During the weekend I learned where the first aid supplies were stored, where the showers were located, and met my fellow corpsmen, but not much more. Monday morning I started work for the Marine Reconnaissance Battalion. My introduction to the special units was rappelling (sliding down a rope) from a helicopter. I intimated it was not my first time so I would be less conspicuous as a Corpsman among special Marines, and found myself, terrifyingly, being pushed out the back of a helicopter a hundred feet in the air, attached by a couple of flimsy ropes. It was so noisy and windy that it was almost impossible to hear the life-protecting instructions by the Rappel Master that were helping me depart. Fortunately, all went well and I was almost immediately standing on the ground with well-wishers and support staff helping me un-tether myself.

This dramatic introduction to leadership training in the

military instilled in me the importance of trusting in the ability of those around me to do their job effectively. I had just put my life in their hands and they had delivered admirably. They were most experienced with the job at hand, and knew the most about how to get it done properly. This lesson has stayed with me throughout my life. If you want to know about how something is done by the staff around you...ask! Not only are they the experts, but if the person has pride in what he does, he will be more than happy to share the details with you.

I also learned that leaders protect their people. The Rappel Master was tasked with ensuring everyone did their jobs effectively and that participants would not die—no small task! As leaders, everyone on that team extended protection to the participants and felt a deep sense of responsibility for the continued existence and functionality of their followers—something for which I, as a participant, am extremely grateful.

With trust and protection, a safe environment is created where authentic relationships can form and become the foundation for success. Rappel Masters are most effective when they have relationships with the people involved. Whether it is fellow leaders in the exercise or those that are the recipients of the training, the Rappel Master must have a sufficient understanding of where uncertainty or lack of focus could have dire consequences.

In the case of my first rappelling experience, the Rappel Master anticipated my inexperience and unbeknownst to me had alerted the rappel team to take extra precautions. A good leader will work hard to understand the activities and abilities of the team to ensure team members are capable and poised for success. Only through developing a relationship that is deep enough can a leader accurately estimate current capabilities and attitudes. Occasionally, when a leader doesn't have this depth of understanding, she must provide a safety net to ensure that a person she doesn't know well is protected from harm.

My job in the military required that I know my fellow team members well. During this period of learning, my job was to take care of injured or ill members of the small unit to which I was assigned. I was highly trained in the ability to render first aid and care in all types of environments, but in reality, my job did not begin until something had gone wrong in the preparation and execution of specific activities. So, I felt the best way to do my job was to know the people around me well enough to see where potential problems might occur.

By extension, this could only come from learning about my peers, leaders and subordinates through individual relationships with each of them. Getting to know them well enough to know what was "normal," allowed me to better see when conditions were "abnormal". Without this knowledge, I would have been ineffective as a medical caregiver and later as a leader. Also, since there were many activities we undertook that could have dire consequences, I worked hard to become a leader that could use this relationship-gained information to actively protect those under my leadership.

One operation entailed building a rope bridge across a stream to transport people and supplies to the other side. This practice exercise was scheduled for a night that saw torrential rain throughout the day and falling temperatures. The river to be crossed was beyond flood stage, so a decision was made early in the day to delay the activity until conditions improved. Unfortunately, the Platoon Commander decided to go ahead and did not inform either of the corpsmen on site. I was awakened in the late evening to loud calls of "Corpsmen Up" – the traditional call that medical help is needed immediately. Throwing on clothes and traversing the swollen river in a rubber boat, I came upon a scene where the Platoon Commander was exhausted to the point of collapse and his buddy, a Marine Sergeant, was floating face-down in the water and not breathing. After performing CPR for more than a couple hours while transporting these two men from the bank of a river, in a rubber boat, in the back of a truck and finally in an ambulance, the Sergeant was pronounced dead from drowning. The Platoon Commander survived, but barely. I ultimately ended up having to attend the funeral of the Sergeant in Arlington National Cemetery. This was a hard lesson in leadership that I never forgot; if you are responsible for someone, take the necessary steps to protect them. Had I known the Platoon Commander might proceed in the face of detrimental conditions, I might have saved a life. My relationship with him was distant and my understanding of his nature insufficient to avert these dire consequences.

My unit's job was to gather information and not get caught. It was dangerous work, as we were going in and out of places that were generally remote and hard to access. This made it critical for us to be at the top of our game in our abilities, preparation, and teamwork.

Working in these teams on such dangerous assignments taught me that each person brought a valuable set of skills to the activities being undertaken. Knowing how those skills worked together to form a comprehensive set of capabilities and understanding the level of competence of each person was critical. It was in the team's best interest for each of us to be very good at our jobs, to be comfortable in our abilities, and to be engaged. In order to effectively lead the team, the leader had to know how these skills worked together and complemented one another. Of course, relationships between the members of the team played another large role in success, so knowing each member individually was only part of the job—knowing the status of relationships *between* team members was also vital.

My military experience ingrained in me the importance of relationships in the workplace and how I, as a leader, choreographed the critical activities to be conducted, through my knowledge and participation in these relationships.

How the military differs from the civilian community

The goal of the military fighting force is success in war. Survival, life or death, is dependent on the person next to you being good at what they do. It was very clear early-on that I could not survive on my own talents, efforts, desires, etc. My life was clearly dependent on the people with whom I worked—leaders, peers, and subordinates. This is the natural scheme of life in the military, but it's very different from life in the civilian world. In the civilian world, it is unusual to place your life in someone else's hands. Firefighters, policemen, and some others are the exception, but generally, the civilian workplace is less hazardous than the military environment. So, there is not the imperative to have the person next to you or working for you, be your key dependent for survival. Yet, in a way it is imperative because if a team is to perform at maximum capacity, your livelihood depends on the expertise and success of those around you. Taking the time to develop strong relationships rewards the leader with a top-performing team.

Efficiency is another aspect of relationships that differs between the military and civilian life. The military environment is one of frequent starting over. Every three years or less, military members were reassigned to a different unit or post. Since the age of 18, I have lived in more than 15 places around the country and around the world. Because of this constant movement, the immediacy of forming relationships was a constant pressure and crucial to fostering leadership success. The bonds we formed tended to be quick, deep, and in many cases did not last for long. Good or bad, they were very different from the relationship one might have with a neighbor over 30 years of living next door to one another. Leaders in the military have to have efficient ways to meet someone and know a bit about them and their abilities right off the bat.

In order to facilitate the quick development of relationships, the military uses visual clues. A rank insignia shows how they fit in the structure; ribbons and insignia on their uniform show schools they have attended and where they have been in different campaigns; and medals show where they have been specifically recognized for their talents or success. If only we had these clues in civilian life! Instead, forming relationships can be harder and take more time and energy to learn about someone. In civilian life, we have to be present, aware, and make an effort to invest the time.

The military also taught me that you can only go as fast as your slowest team member. Once accepted, this premise identifies where the bulk of your leadership must be focused to improve a team. Investing in the ability of those that are not sufficiently skilled is imperative. Unfortunately, the military also differs in that it is almost impossible to remove someone who is not sufficiently capable. So, the effort invested in poor performers becomes much more extensive.

The strongest teams are those that recognize the individual value of each person and work hard to improve that value, thus improving the team. I think this is very similar in both environments since people are people, some fast and some slow. Because of circumstances in the military, there is a greater pressure to improve the pace or expertise of a team's weakest members. If you choose to improve the weaker performers, you can experience the benefit of heightened efforts to improve your team in the civilian sector as well.

What I learned in the military carried through my transition to civilian life. Good or bad, my approach with relationships and the responsibility I feel as a leader has strong military underpinnings that I continue to follow. My approach has served me well:

- my success is dependent on the skill and commitment of those around me (which I can foster through trust and protection)
- although it takes more time and energy to develop relationships than previously, it is well worth the effort
- a team performs only as well as its weakest member
- no matter how it feels, easy or hard, the result is a much stronger team when the relationships are solid.

Any success I have achieved through leadership has come through focusing on others and helping them to be successful. This is the one fundamental I pursue each day. With a team, it's not about me; it's about the team members. Through this approach, I have achieved far more knowledge, understanding, achievement and loyalty than I ever expected.

Steps for Building Successful Relationships in the Workplace

Step 1: Know those around you

Pay attention to how you introduce yourself to the team and new team members to each other. Taking the time for a positive introduction will set the stage for all future interactions between a leader and the superiors, peers and staff around him. I have found a number of methods work in establishing the foundation for an effective relationship. The approach identified as MBWA–management by walking around—is still effective.

Taking the time to have conversations demonstrates your genuine interest in a staff member's life, successes and challenges and helps to develop the common ground for working together. This also communicates a clear message that your role as a leader includes caring about a person and being willing to approach them in their workspace and listen to what they have to say.

Step 2: Learn what they do

One of your first steps as a leader must be to gain a clear understanding of what the people around you do and how well they do it. In order to most effectively coordinate and maximize team efforts, you'll need to know whether or not they are interested in, skilled at, and comfortable (or even happy!) with their role. Build your relationship with your staff by asking questions about what is going well, what things might be improved, and what activities are done by someone else and "delivered" to a person for additional work.

Most teams function in a process environment where they receive work from someone else and are asked to take a specific action to add value prior to delivering their output elsewhere. Understanding how a person feels about their role in this process can help develop the bond needed for effective leadership. Also, when you can determine if a person is not comfortable or capable in their position, you can take action to solve this problem.

Teams that perform well are those that have members who want to do good work and understand their role and how it fits in to the overall process–bigger picture. Through interest, learning about a person and sharing some of yourself–developing a relationship—a leader can see how to effectively care about staff and coordinate their efforts.

Step 3: Build trust

Effective leaders must establish trust. Some of this can be done through one-on-one relationships, but trust also comes from general, every day activity in the workplace. Following through, being dependable, protecting confidences, and acknowledging values are all ways of building trust. Conducting yourself with this kind of integrity—and expecting it from your team members—is a visible sign of respect.

I always have an open-door policy. Staff members can stop in and share ideas and feelings without fear of having them revealed and with the certainty that their thoughts will be carefully considered. This is two-way trust. Creating a safe environment for people to share their thoughts and concerns shows that I respect the value of their time and that I understand good ideas come from everywhere. "Don't talk the talk if you can't walk the walk"—a leader must live by her word and follow the same guidelines for behavior that are being asked of her team.

Knowledge and experience can be used as a powerful tool in the workplace—a tool for good or evil. When used to expand the capacity of those around you, knowledge can help build smart and productive employees and teams. When used as a weapon, it builds fear and mistrust of the person wielding the power. I have always worked to invest in others by sharing what I have learned along my journey. Sometimes the lessons are ignored. Sometimes they are embraced. Either way the value is two-fold. First, you are giving your time to help another understand you. This helps to strengthen the relationship. Second, you are trying to expand the knowledge and understanding of another and, even if they are not receptive, they are aware of the effort. The best result is when you help someone understand something you have learned and they embrace it and apply it in a real-world situation.

People that have leaders willing to share their journey and its lessons feel valued and respond with a high level of commitment. When a leader is unwilling to share information or experience, an employee feels left in the dark and unaware of the potential discussions or decisions that are ongoing around him, which may have a direct impact on his future. This undervalues employees and can easily create a climate of uncertainty and lack of motivation. If you want to build a strong team, share as much information about yourself and anything that impacts your team and their work as you can. Staff will feel included, valued, and respond with incredible performance.

Hiring a pending, Master's- level statistics graduate sorely needing a job, led to one of the best leadership experiences I have had. New to the workforce, I took this fellow under my wing and taught him all I could about our business. Since he had been immersed in the education system, there were no preconceived ideas that intruded on his learning, and when sufficiently prepared, I asked him to turn his focus on applying his talents to the work goals. The relationship then became a valuable two-way effort, as I worked to understand his approaches and he worked to propose how they might fit the current business circumstances. We trusted one another, because we each invested the best we had to offer. This

Relationship

investment led to deep trust and a very strong relationship of mutual interest and amazing results. .

Step 4: Protect your people

Protecting your people can be a big challenge for leaders. Too much protection stifles the learning process where team members need to take action and be responsible to grow. After all, we learn the most from making mistakes...and recovering from them. Too little protection can allow a person to be isolated from the team and leader, perhaps even expose people to negative consequences that are catastrophic. A good leader protects the team to a correct level, so growth occurs and bad outcomes do not. This comes from experience, but it is significantly easier if you have strong relationships with your team and a deeper level of understanding about when they are secure or when they are vulnerable. Instances in the military led me to be extremely aware of the need for protection.

I had the opportunity to attempt to save 11 individual lives while in the service. Fortunately, I was successful on 8 occasions. The most difficult day of my life was when I stood in Arlington National Cemetery in Washington, DC while they buried one of my "failures". Although my medical advice was sought prior to the event that took this soldier's life, weather conditions were so unfavorable during the incident as to ensure failure, and my advice was ultimately ignored. At the gravesite in Arlington, the parents of this highly skilled and successful Marine asked me why I let him die. I had no good answer and agonized about the situation for years. Perhaps it was this event that made me so committed to caring for and protecting those around me as a leader.

Leaders in the workplace must build solid relationships so

they can appropriately protect their staff. To prevent providing protection that stifles your team, focus on doing whatever is necessary to help your staff to be successful and comfortable in their jobs.

Step 5: Foster success

Fostering success means making sure you have the right people, in the right place, at the right time, with the right skills and information. There are cases where an employee, or even a peer, may not be in the right position. This could be due to their attitude, their abilities, or external forces, but something is undermining their success. This usually means a leader has a responsibility to help them appreciate that they are not in the right job, or perhaps not even in the right company. If this is the case, try to approach the situation without negative judgment, to the greatest extent possible. If you can develop a strong relationship, and you can see that someone is not in the right position, if they trust and respect you, you can help them find a situation for which they are better suited.

I was in a civilian position where it was made clear in the interview process that I had to have the capacity to fire an employee. This was just the first of a few jobs that I've held that valued the decisiveness needed to carry out hard staffing decisions. In this case, a supervisor had been promoted to manager and I realized almost immediately that this person didn't have the attitude and capability to be a manager. She was miserable, but couldn't understand why. Over a period of months and through one-on-one discussions, we came to understand that she was not comfortable with the level of responsibility she had. She was uncertain what decisions to make and her increasing concern over taking the correct action was undermining her staff and her performance. Ultimately, we agreed that this role was not for her and moved her back to supervisory duties. She was happier, the company was happier, and because we took the time to investigate alternatives prior to making the decision, her trust and respect for me remained intact.

Increasingly, I see a lack of commitment from leaders, especially senior leaders, to recognize the value of relationships. These leaders manage people like they would equipment and supplies, rather than nurturing relationships. This is probably because it's much easier to manage commodities than it is to effectively relate to people. However, in order to achieve extraordinary, lasting results, leaders *must* take the time to build relationships. If a leader is uncomfortable with working to help people succeed, he should not be in a leadership position. Unfortunately, achieving results through relationship-building seems to be minority thinking in today's business community.

And Beyond

As a final consideration and with some thoughts for new leaders, let me ask you this: *Does being a leader require that you are in a position of authority?* Much of business leadership has been built on a formal structure of responsibility with commensurate authority—the traditional, hierarchical organizational chart. Increasingly, however, this is not the case. Flatter organizations, matrix management, and project-oriented activities have created situations where much of the time the person who is stepping up to lead a group or activity is not necessarily the person with formal authority over the team.

When a leader has formal authority over a team, building strong relationships is important, but he always has the "last resort". If someone on the team doesn't perform up to standard, you have the power to remove them from employment. Just as in the military, I believe that having to fall back on the "last resort"–having to use rank or power to get something accomplished—is tantamount to failure. If a leader nurtures the relationships with his staff, firing can usually be avoided. However, with the authority, you do have that power if you need it.

Without this level of authority over a workgroup, relationships become even more important since you likely won't have the ability to just get rid of someone who isn't performing. Leadership is all about getting people to follow your direction, and coordinate efforts to complete an objective. When you demonstrate as a leader that you care about the people on the team and the quality and outcome of the work, it encourages team members to cooperate and align their efforts—even though you are not in a position of direct authority. Personal relationships are the basis for this influence. Care about those with whom you are working and extend an interest in what they do and how it is done, to effectively orchestrate the talent around you.

For new leaders

Being a leader can be stimulating—and frightening. A piece of advice that I have taught to others, and work to follow, is to lead by listening. A new leader can develop strong relationships by working hard at getting to know the people around him, both peers (for experience) and staff (for abilities). Being curious about what interests staff and what they can do, combined with showing concern for each person's well-being, will help achieve your goals as a young leader. Building relationships will foster your growth in the position and give you a well-rounded knowledge of the workplace. This growth and knowledge will foster leadership success.

Closing thought

I learned some hard lessons in the military that have served me well in civilian life. Any success I have achieved is due to the good work of the many people I have been privileged to lead over the years. This success was grounded in the relationships that were built on trust and respect gained through daily interaction. Challenge yourself each day to focus on the success of others rather than on yourself. If you want to build a strong and lasting relationship, concentrate your efforts on the other person and commit to their success. The fruits of your efforts will pay off in the end: you'll gain knowledge, understanding, loyalty and success (for you and your team) beyond your imagination. The next step toward leadership success is as close as your next interaction—it happens one conversation at a time.

CHAPTER 10: RELATIONSHIPS IN THE FAMILY OF GOD

BY CASEY PETERSON

"I'm so glad, I'm a part, of the family of God.

I've been washed in the fountain, cleansed by His blood.

Joint heirs with Jesus, as we travel this sod.

For I'm a part of the family,

the Family of God."

I learned this hymn as a young child, a young innocent child who saw the family of God as a healthy family, simply learning how to love God and love others together. When I think of this song now, I see boundaries between churches...that each church sees itself as the family of God. If you have relationships within your church, serve within your church by getting 'plugged in' (as we say) to ministry—you are active in the family of God.

Relationship

I see our Family of God as a much larger community; however, my experiences within different denominations paint a different story that I'd like to share. My hope in sharing this story is that our relationships within the family of God would be stronger, that we'd overcome a false sense of lack of unity in our faith due to denomination segregation.

Let me start by sharing that my background in church families is somewhat diverse. I was baptized as an infant in the Lutheran church, raised in a small non-denominational church, and then I attended multiple churches in high school. I served in a ministry called Campus Life, so I attended with my friends at multiple churches—Nazarene, Catholic, Episcopalian, Baptist, Lutheran, United Church of Christ, Assembly of God and multiple non-denominational. I always felt that if I was with people, if I was applying God's Word and submitting my life to Him, that it didn't really matter what church I attended. I enjoyed worshiping God with my friends and serving alongside them. I think this is maybe because that song always stuck in my mind, that we are all a part of the Family of God, regardless of where we go on Sunday morning.

I attended an Assembly of God church for about 14 years, where I was baptized as an adult. It was in this church body where I learned what true Fellowship was like and served the church and community. I was involved in facilitating Small Groups, Women's Ministry, Children's Ministry, MOPS and had amazing Christian Women disciple me. It wasn't a perfect church, but I respect the model of being a church member and serving in a primary church. There is a great comfort in the relationships that you grow within a church community.

When I think of relationships that are most meaningful in my life, I think of those that I have developed during service within a church community. Those people who I have done Bible Studies with and we have worked together. I've seen God 'show up', if you will, answer prayers right before my eyes! It's an incredible experience to work along side others, pray with them, weep with them, and rejoice with them. Romans 12 is rich with context in how we should be loving each other:

Romans 12: Love in Action *⁹ Love must be sincere. Hate what is evil; cling to what is good. ¹⁰ Be devoted to one another in love. Honor one another above yourselves. ¹¹ Never be lacking in zeal, but keep your spiritual fervor, serving the Lord. ¹² Be joyful in hope, patient in affliction, faithful in prayer. ¹³ Share with the Lord's people who are in need. Practice hospitality. ¹⁴ Bless those who persecute you; bless and do not curse. ¹⁵ Rejoice with those who rejoice; mourn with those who mourn. ¹⁶ Live in harmony with one another. Do not be proud, but be willing to associate with people of low position. Do not be conceited. ¹⁷ Do not repay anyone evil for evil. Be careful to do what is right in the eyes of everyone. ¹⁸ If it is possible, as far as it depends on you, live at peace with everyone.*

This is love in action, in relationships, within and outside of church walls. We are to have love in action. I have served in shelters, attended Celebrate Recovery meetings, seen people raw, broken, crushed and hurting but also shining in their hope in Christ so brightly. God is everywhere, in each interaction we have with people. Others have blessed me so incredibly, especially when I was supposed to be the one helping them! That's how God works when we weep with those who weep and rejoice with those who rejoice, He just shows up and we get to witness His plan right before our eyes.

Knowing that God is everywhere and He will use us in any situation and relationship, my husband and I trusted Him in our moving our family to another state. We moved to a very small community with one established Christian church building, which happened to be a Southern Baptist denomination. My best friend had been attending there and we had instant fellowship through her relationships. We didn't really research doctrine differences with Southern

Baptist compared with Assembly of God, they both felt like community Bible-teaching churches. We "plugged in" to ministry right away by serving in multiple areas of the church. My husband and I both served in AWANA, I helped in MOPPETS (caring for children while their mothers attended MOPS meetings) and then became a Mentor Mom for MOPS (Mothers of Preschoolers). I led MOPS Bible Studies for about three years, and began coordinating a Discipleship Program which grew to a dozen women and also personally Discipled three MOPS moms (mentoring them in their faith). My husband was involved in Worship Team and acted as a Youth Ministry Leader. I only tell you of our service so you know that we were actively trying to connect into the church family and serve in our new community.

After about four years at the church, I think we realized that we didn't fit into the culture of the church...not that we don't fit into the Family of God. There is a reason that there are so many church denominations, that there are different cultures within. They all serve a greater purpose to glorify God, but they all do them in unique ways to meet different needs. It doesn't mean that we can't partner together and still work together, it just means that we may worship differently.

However, this experience has opened my eyes to some interesting church biases. Upon leaving the church, we didn't meet with the Pastor or say anything formal, as it was more of a personal decision, and it wasn't as if we wanted to give him feedback to change anything. I continued to serve in mid-week activities twice a week and supported ministries. My kids were still going to these mid-week activities, so of course I would continue to serve in them. I wasn't saying no to God or the relationships that I'd made in these ministries, I was just saying no to the Sunday culture of the Baptist church. At least that was what I thought.

I think most of the time when people leave a church, it's due to dissention, a conflict that is irreconcilable, or some horrible scandal that we've all heard about on TV. It is probably more rare to leave under our circumstances: to leave with respect for differences in worship and style, respect for ministries provided to the community and still love the church members. It is interesting to see the dynamics of people when you stop attending 'their' church. We got quite a mixed reaction. I don't think people knew what to do, so they didn't do anything. Very few asked. No one called. And relationships dwindled. There was the handful of those who seemed to care and want to maintain a relationship, but the family of God broke down in this picture. The feelings of rejection overcame the feelings of love that God calls us to aside from our denomination. We are the body of Christ, the Family of God, regardless of the church that we attend.

Many churches believe that if you "do it differently" than they do, it's wrong. There are many beliefs within Christian churches that cause diversity and differences. They aren't wrong, they are just different and we should respect their differences. When we make other believers feel like what they are doing is wrong because they worship differently, it is not healthy for our family of God. It hurts our relationships and is a bad example for others considering our faith. I think I need to be as sensitive to those who feel I've 'left them' who feel I'm judging their form of worship, as much as I feel they are judging my not doing things their way.

When I read Romans 12 on service in the Body of Christ, I see the picture of the Family of God as a child, the larger community of believers.

"Humble Service in the Body of Christ[3] For by the grace given me;1 say to every one of you: Do not think of yourself more highly than you ought, but rather think of yourself with sober judgment, in accordance with the faith God has distributed to each of you.[4] For just as each of us has one body with many members, and these members do not all have the same function,[5] so in Christ we, though many, form one body, and each member belongs to all the others.[6] We have different gifts, according to the grace given to each of us. If your gift is

prophesying,then prophesy in accordance with your faith;[7] if it is serving, then serve; if it is teaching, then teach;[8] if it is to encourage, then give encouragement;if it is giving, then give generously;if it is to lead,do it diligently; if it is to show mercy, do it cheerfully." Romans 12

I love that the first portion of this is humility, to humbly serve each other in the family, and to not think of anyone more important than the other in the family. Secondly, we are all a part of the family of God, the body of Christ, each with different roles and purposes by which He is revealing to us, in every interaction, in every moment that we are doing anything with other people! When we interact with anyone, we have an opportunity to glorify God. This scripture is typically shared in churches when Pastors need people to serve in ministry, fulfill roles within the church. While I think that is valid, I think God is calling us to a much bigger "macro" perspective as a Christian body of Christ. I wonder how powerfully we could serve the world if all of our congregations united and put aside some of the differences.

I've seen these relationships played out successfully in multiple churches in a small community where leaders worked together in ministries to reach out. In this community, Vacation Bible Schools were facilitated by members of multiple congregations, one church had a MOPS group and the another hosted AWANA, each meeting needs for the entire community of families—not just their own members—and combining resources of leaders in ministry areas. There weren't boundaries (caused by church denominations), when it came to loving God and loving others for Christ. I've seen the other side, where, if you don't go to this church, you don't serve in "our ministries" as we don't know if you believe the way we do, even if you go to another Christian church. Why the relationship break-down? Aren't we all in this together?

I am not a perfect member of the church family, in fact, I'm quiet the contrary, in my opinion. I rely on Christ's strength and frequently am thankful to review the scripture that "when

I am weak, then I am strong" (2 Corinthians 12:10). It comforts me to know that He can use my weaknesses, faults and experiences and use them for His glory if I allow Him. That's the entire point of sharing a testimony a lot of time, to show how God can take something awful and allow us to bring Him glory through it, encourage others or give them hope when they face the same challenge.

That's how we work together in our ideal Family of God, encouraging others when we are feeling weak, looking beyond organizational boundaries defined by church denominations, and asking God to show us how to love one another as we read so clearly in Romans 12. My prayer is that we become a living sacrifice so we hear what God wants us to do, and do it. I think we just get in His way a lot of the time, with our own self-doubts and wondering "why?"—when we should just trust and obey and submit to his will, His good, pleasing and perfect will.

Romans 12: A Living Sacrifice*Therefore, I urge you, brothers and sisters, in view of God's mercy, to offer your bodies as a living sacrifice, holy and pleasing to God—this is your true and proper worship. ² Do not conform to the pattern of this world, but be transformed by the renewing of your mind. Then you will be able to test and approve what God's will is—his good, pleasing and perfect will.*

CHAPTER 11: RELATIONSHIP AND ADDICTION

BY HEATHER LARSON

5 Some time later, Jesus went up to Jerusalem for one of the Jewish festivals. 2 Now there is in Jerusalem near the Sheep Gate a pool, which in Aramaic is called Bethesda [a] and which is surrounded by five covered colonnades. 3 Here a great number of disabled people used to lie—the blind, the lame, the paralyzed. 4 [b] 5 One who was there had been an invalid for thirty-eight years. 6 When Jesus saw him lying there and learned that he had been in this condition for a long time, he asked him, "Do you want to get well?"

7 "Sir," the invalid replied, "I have no one to help me into the pool when the water is stirred. While I am trying to get in, someone else goes down ahead of me."

8 Then Jesus said to him, "Get up! Pick up your mat and walk." John 5:1-8

I have often used these scriptures in regard to addictions of all types to illustrate not only the need to recognize this disease, but to choose a way out as well. People sometimes have difficulty acknowledging alcoholism, chemical dependency, gambling, sexual addiction, etc. as an illness, yet those that are caught in these strongholds reveal that sometimes the harder they try to get well, the sicker they seem to become. It is as if an invisible force holds them captive, much like the man beside the pool in the Bible story.

Addiction thrives in an atmosphere of isolation, loneliness, and fear. There is an expression repeated often in recovery groups that "an addict alone, is in bad company." In other words, addicts need intimacy with others in order to survive the painful process of healing. Twelve-step groups, sponsors to guide and be accountable to, people to hear our deepest feelings and places to process them are crucial to get well. Relationships where transparency is possible helps to form friendships that may last for a lifetime. Most importantly, an intimate relationship with God is vital in order for addicts to heal.

I am a recovering addict who has worked a program of recovery for thirty-three years. I began using amphetamines as a teenager and continued for approximately fifteen years. I am the youngest of a family of ten children, many of whom struggled with various addictions. My childhood was filled with the usual positive and negative experiences, yet as I grew into my teen years I experienced loneliness and fear on a regular basis, as well as a need to perform or wear a "good girl" mask. I was always the girl others could confide in but no one knew my authentic self because I could not risk exposure of any weaknesses to others. Mixing this with a desire to be thin and "beautiful," I developed a secret world. I could not confide in anyone (an addict alone is in bad company), nor could I seem to gain freedom, and it took that very same friend as the man by the pool in need of healing to come alongside and encourage me to choose life and recovery. Jesus has been my friend and healer in every possible way. His faithfulness has been unending.

Acknowledging dependency is, of course, the first step and it is huge. To finally admit and tell trusted people my secrets seemed almost impossible. Another common expression in recovery, "you're as sick as your secrets," rang true for me, and as I revealed my heart and shared intimate details of my life I began to heal miraculously. My new friend, Jesus, whom I had met at a local revival meeting, walked with me through each step. This, combined with Christian twelve-step meeting, changed my world completely. No longer was I afraid and lonely. My best friend, Jesus, was with me continuously. I met with others in need of healing who understood my life and met with me—sometimes on a daily basis. These were kindred spirits you might say, unexpected friends who have helped to mold and shape my life just by making themselves available.

Lack of intimacy was the culprit in my life—a chasm so deep, a void that I could not fill no matter how hard I tried. It seemed that no matter how many acquaintances, accomplishments or accolades I received, I still refused to let even one person know of my inward struggles for fear of rejection.

True intimacy in relationship with others involves a freedom to be ourselves no matter what the issues may be. Just *being* is enough—no pretenses, no ego, no puffing ourselves up—just *being* and reveling in that.

Approximately twenty-five years ago I began working in the field of chemical dependency as a counselor. I have worked with hundreds of people, either in recovery groups or individual counseling. A common denominator with many people is a need for intimacy in personal relationships as well as a need to have a sense of significance. To give and receive is paramount for healing. I have often jokingly told folks that their "receivers" were broken. In other words, like my former self, they can give to others, yet have a difficult time receiving for themselves. In order for balance to be in a person's life there must be an ability to master both the giving of self and receiving others unto yourself. This is a tall order for those of us who have hidden behind masks to keep others at bay. Slowly but surely, the masks of self-sufficiency, pride, and ego must go so that which remains is real and truthful.

Honesty is much prized in recovery, since dishonesty pervades most addicts' lives. Repeatedly addicts are encouraged to work "an honest program" because their existence has been predicated on lie after lie as a means to survive the lifestyle of addiction. Few relationships can survive the harsh reality that true friends are hard to come by in a (drug) using community. New relationships built on truth and trust allow for intimacy to develop as the addict grows and changes daily.

Recovering addicts are probably the most fascinating people I know. Beside the fact that research finds this population of people to generally be of above-average intelligence, they are the most amazingly creative folks I have met. Once addicts make a commitment to recovery, the growth and change in their lives and relationships is rapid and steady as they continue on the right path.

Even as I traveled my own difficult journey with addiction and found healing, even more challenging, perhaps, has been dealing with my son, Gary's, addiction. It seemed that God was preparing me to handle much more than just my personal battles, He was arming me for a full-blown war to help save my son's life.

My Son

My oldest son, Gary, began experimenting with drugs at age thirteen. He is forty-seven years old today and has been my greatest source of inspiration and education as I observed the progression of his disease throughout the years. His struggles were one of the reasons I chose the field of chemical dependency as a profession.

First, I'll fill you in with some background. Forty-four years ago I married a wonderful man who had sole custody of his three-year-old son, Gary. He was a beautiful blonde-haired cherub whose biological mother was unable to care for him because of her own issues. My husband fought for custody and I legally adopted Gary on his fourth birthday. Due to his mother's extreme neglect during his short life, he experienced trauma, for which he was medicated. When I came into the picture, a nineteen-year-old struggling with her own problems, I became instant mom to a child I loved, but had absolutely no idea how to cope with. Those were tough years laced with the birth of three more children, lack of financial security, and eventually facing the teen years with a child who had become rebellious and well on his way to addiction.

It was during Gary's first forty-six day treatment program that I became educated about the disease of chemical dependency, for him, and for myself as well. One of the first truths I learned was that this was a three-fold disease: physical, emotional and spiritual.

The physical aspect involves a genetic component along with the "right" combination of an individual's brain chemicals. In other words, the inherited characteristics were already present in our son. Kind of like dry powdered milk—you just add water to it and you have the full blown product. Gary's predisposition was in place when he experimented with his first drug.

As far as the emotional component goes, Gary had the odds against him in that area as well with a biological mother who abandoned him, the loss of his beloved grandparents, and a mom and dad who were ill-equipped to help him. This "perfect storm" of traumatic events led to years of sadness and confusion, and was also a set-up for addictions.

Finally, our entire family was spiritually depleted, unable to make positive changes due to a lack of direction. It takes a spiritual key to unlock the doors of addiction.

Throughout my years of counseling I encountered only a few clients who could even come close to experiencing the trials that we observed our son endure. The progression of his disease led to repeated offenses and incarcerations, several car accidents and one serious suicide attempt. Our home became a place of intense grief for a family that longed for a miracle, as year after year we experienced a range of emotions regarding Gary.

Chemical dependency is a family disease. Each family member is affected, taking on different roles to survive and progressing through the various stages of grief. Several of our other children became angry and we all ultimately had to separate from him in order to live healthy lives.

Chemical dependency, alcoholism, and addictions in general are definitely not conducive to establishing intimate relationships. Our son's preoccupation with drugs and manipulative ways created a huge wedge between our family members. His father and I dreaded his phone calls, yet feared the times we didn't hear from him.

One year ago Gary reached the bottom of his pit when his addicted wife committed suicide by overdosing on prescription pills. Although they were bonded through "using," they also shared a great love for one another. Gary was devastated. He had nothing to lean on, as his wife was gone and he was homeless as well. His father and I stayed close through agonizing days and nights of grief until he entered yet another treatment center. He had been to at least six centers prior to this. This time he was serious. He was sick and tired of being sick and tired. He is almost one year clean today-the first time in over thirty years. He is involved in daily Narcotic Anonymous meetings, has surrendered his life to God and his transformation is miraculous. Our cup runneth over!

Our family is in the process of being restored after so many years of separation. Gary is living in a clean and sober house for men, and he calls daily to tell us about all the new relationships he is forming. These are true friends in every way, looking out for one another like the members of the early church in the Book of Acts in the Bible. Recently Gary shared with me that there is a table in their meeting hall where anyone who would like to can bring shoes, clothing or anything useful to be picked up by someone in need. Truly these relationships are as deep, intimate and faithful as I have seen.

Lives and relationships can be restored, even after the most devastating events in a person's life—but it requires making a choice. Like the man sitting by the pool in need of healing, an individual must decide to take the first step. I often tell folks that healing or recovery will not just "fall onto them." In other words, healing comes when one believes that it is possible and trusts in the One who has the power to intervene. When this happens the hope and joy for a bright future is at hand as they enter into the plan that God has for them. Life becomes brand new as the old ways truly pass away and the healing takes place.

A Discussion with Heather

Paul: I want to start out by asking you how you got into counseling.

Heather: I got into counseling when our son was in treatment at a local treatment center. It was during that time that I began to understand recovery. I started doing a Bible study with the adolescents there, and I did that for a year.

Then I began taking my [counseling] classes. I went back to school because I had tried college after high school, but I just wasn't interested. So I looked into becoming a Chemical Dependency Counselor. I started taking classes, and some of the staff at the (my son's) treatment center were in the classes. Eventually, they asked me if I would come to work for them because they had known me from that year I was doing the Bible study. I became a counselor-in-training and I finished my schooling while I was getting paid.

So God had first gone before me, and opened the door for me to do the Bible studies. The kids were very open and a lot of them came to the Lord. I also had Bible studies with them outside of treatment for years and am still in touch with some of them.

Paul: What year was that?

Heather: That would have been '80 maybe '83. So they are grown up now and have kids of their own.

Paul: Yes, getting older themselves.

Heather: Yes. I would take them camping and spend a lot of time with them...a group of those teenagers.

So our son went through the program and I learned recovery. I knew the Lord and I was a studying the Bible but I didn't understand how it related to recovery until I got into the program. And then it all became clear that they are one and the same. You know, there's not any difference really.

Paul: Tell me about that.

Heather: Well, in the program of AA or Narcotics Anonyms or any of the 12-step programs they talk about a higher power and they also use the 12 steps to heal. But the first step is recognizing that you have an addiction and the second one is believing that God can restore you... a power greater than yourself. The third step is to turn your will and your life over to God. Then you begin to understand him. In the program, a lot of people don't understand who God is and they may not have had a Christian upbringing. So often their higher power becomes the group or something that is greater than them until they come to a place of accepting God. Coming to the Lord is about surrender, and recovery is totally about surrender. Without surrender there won't be any healing or any recovery. It is a process, of course.

Paul: Yes.

Heather: They're one and the same.

Paul: I'm wondering whether, over the years, you have seen a connection between relationship and addiction.

Heather: Usually, by the time I have met people that are in need of healing, they are depleted. They have lost families, lost relationships, lost jobs, lost most everything before they are ready to change. It's not always that severe, but more often you meet people that are at the bottom because now they have either been court ordered or their life has fallen apart so much that they need help. They have lost most of their relationships and the relationships they have formed in the "using" world are not relationships that they can count on. That old saying there is no loyalty among thieves, well, there really isn't. You really don't have anybody you can call "friend." And so, by the time I've seen them they are without anything. They're just depleted in every way.

The "using" affects every relationship because drugs and alcohol cloud the mind and spirit and emotions. So often they are people who lie, who steal, who are manipulative, and not people that you can rely on. Of course, that's in varying degrees with different people, but I don't think I've ever met one addict that didn't say, at some point, they did one or a number of those things.

Paul: Those are anti-relational behaviors.

Heather: Those are not conducive to relationships. Your family may love you, but they don't want you around. Certainly that was the case with our son. We loved him, but dreaded the times that we spent a lot of time with him because there was no intimacy whatsoever. It's all surface. It's all phony and you don't know what's real. You don't know what to believe. I shouldn't say it's all phony because some of it may be real, but you can't decipher that. And so, yes, addicts are typically very lonely. By the time they get to that place they feel lost and alone like the prodigal who's gone out and done it all, spent it all, and ended up with the pigs. But they get to a point where they say, "I've had enough. I'm sick and tired of being sick and tired."

And then they make a choice. It does not happen overnight, and they have to give up the old relationships, the old people, places and things because they'll pull you right back down. But then it's a slow rebuilding of relationships.

Often, it's not only in the "using" world that addicts have had relationship issues. Often times growing up... this disease is hereditary and so often you see it in the family you come from. In a family where there is addiction, the emotional, spiritual and physical needs have sometimes not been met growing up. You see that often. The apple doesn't fall far from the tree and the disease (addiction) is hereditary. It's progressive and it's fatal. A lot of people don't know that, but that's why it's considered a disease by the American Medical Association. It has to meet those criteria and it does.

Paul: I didn't realize that.

Heather: Yes. Addiction and alcoholism. People often don't think about alcoholism as being fatal. It's usually a slower progression unless there is an accident or something. It's the same disease whether its alcohol or drug addiction. It's known as cross addiction. You can't just go to a different drug, but that is often what addicts do. The progression of addiction is much more rapid when you combine alcohol and drugs. It seems to progress at a much faster rate. That's why we're seeing late stage addict alcoholics in their 20's and 30's, and they are dying young. Before, we might have thought of an alcoholic as the old man who just drank too much, and it was a slow, slow process. Alcohol generally takes a much slower path. But with drugs, and combining the two, they die young.

So you've got this disease which is physical, emotional and spiritual and the physical part is genetic. It's hereditary. The emotional aspect of it is that all your relationships are affected.

Relationship

You may have grown up in that atmosphere, so you're emotionally stunted, and of course your're stunted if you start using at a young age. You stagnate emotionally at the age that you start using. Often you see a 35 year old who acts like a 13 year-old or a 14 year-old. Whatever time they started using, they stay stuck.

And then the spiritual part of it is a block between God, or a higher power, or something greater than you. You do not feel that connection because it's... well, quite frankly, it's blocked by sin. By something that's taken over you and becomes your God. Drugs and alcohol become your God. And so it takes a spiritual key to unlock that door and in my life that was Jesus. And it was pretty immediate once I recognized that. Then the change happened.

Paul: Would you say that these early addicts... that... are they even capable of healthy relationships?

Heather: No. Absolutely not. They are not capable of it because they are not equipped. And because the drugs separate them emotionally. Their very fabric and their character is compromised.

Paul: So they grow up not knowing how to have relationships.

Heather: Yes, right, and dishonesty is a big part of the disease. Over and over in recovery they say, "This is an honest program." Because addicts have learned to lie and deceive others in order to survive. And so, there is a lot of dishonesty. Getting honest is a huge part of recovery. As an addict, your relationships are not built on honesty. There's hiding and lying and covering up so no one knows.

Paul: As a counselor how do you deal with this dishonesty and lying?

Heather: Well, because I started in treatment, I understand it. That's where I start working and that's the best possible place to start. Either they choose to stay or they leave. The ones that choose to stay are serious about recovery. The rest of the group makes sure that they are serious, because they have to be accountable to the group. So the group itself takes care of each other. It's just beautiful to see.

Somebody would get a hold of the program and the recovery concepts and then they would start sharing it, and it was contagious with the new people. Often when they came in they were belligerent and angry. I've never been cussed out so many times in my life. And yet when you broke down their walls, they were loving and sensitive and bright and kind. You would find that, underneath it all, the real person was under there hiding. So, I found them delightful to work with.

Someone who is in recovery is always easier to work with. The more difficult ones are the ones that come in with a huge amount of denial about their disease. You try to teach them and they may not grab hold, and that can be a long process.

I am not confrontive, but when I'm working with someone in treatment, I can be. Working with someone one-on-one, I would work slowly with them until they broke through the denial, or until something happened that they had to make the changes in their lives. But I think that a lot of time and if you're too confrontive they will dig their heels in. It's being led by the Spirit and knowing when. When to say something and when not to. You know, "OK Lord, how do we deal with this today?" and let the Lord lead in that. I would know when it's the right time is to confront or to say…"Let's take a look at this" because denial is huge. Denial is very thick and it's a method of self-protection. And it's hard to break through that.

Paul: Yes.

Heather: It's not easy. Counseling addicts and alcoholics is not an easy profession. I have to say that today, I much prefer just working with people who are ready, people who are spiritual. It's pretty taxing.

Paul: Bringing someone back is hard.

Heather: Very hard.

Paul: Yes.

Heather: Very hard. And I know when I went into this they said "Most counselors don't last more than two years." When you are working with addiction, it's so tough. You have to keep yourself healthy. To say the words that they used when I was taking my classes, "you have to be weller than well yourself" in order to work with people like this, because it takes a lot out of you.

Paul: Yes, that's a good one to remember. I want to go back to about five minutes ago when you said that the group would keep them honest.

Heather: Yes.

Paul: So it sounds to me like there is some relational stuff going on there. Do you want to talk about that?

Heather: Yes. In groups, especially in group therapy, if someone is just...what they would call "B.S.-ing" everyone, it doesn't take long for the others to confront. They don't seem to have a problem with each other doing that. Sometimes gently, sometimes not so gently. That would happen in the group process.

But sometimes, somebody would share at such a deep level that it opened up other people in the group, so that they could feel their feelings. And that would be a beautiful thing to see. I would know when the Holy Spirit was doing something. I would feel that. The Holy Spirit would just come into a group and they wouldn't want to stop when their group time was up. They would just walk out of the group silently, because of how they'd been impacted. Lots of times it was like that with groups. And that was miraculous.

You could see people turning the corner as they related to others and shared their hearts. Once they shared their hearts with one another they couldn't really take it back. They couldn't say, "Oh I was just joking about that yesterday." The others had heard it and now knew. "You're busted." "Your cover is blown." So they would then get used to sharing at that level, and they would want to share. Where before, during their using, they were busy covering up, now they were opening up. And that goes on after they leave treatment.

That's part of the treatment process when they are in therapy groups. But as they go on to Twelve Step it's the same thing. They share their hearts. They talk. They listen. They get encouraged by one another. They call it "sharing a message of hope" and that is so like Christianity. We share a message of hope, and the others often feel a calling to go on and share that message with other people who are still using and they are available to help people.

If you're in a world of trouble and you want help, boy, you just call AA, NA or one of the Twelve Step groups and somebody will be there to help you. Because that's how they are. They are all about helping people come out of addiction.

Paul: It sounds so relational.

Heather: Yes. Very. And, in order to succeed in recovery, you need to have a sponsor, somebody that you meet with one-on-one, who you do your "step work" with. And that person hears your day to day struggles and gives you homework. That person just walks alongside you through recovery. Your sponsor is really vital to your recovery. I haven't known anybody to recover for any length of time who doesn't 1) have a sponsor and 2) attend meetings on a regular basis. If they work the Twelve Steps and they don't do those two things, they're not likely to make it. It's a commitment, it's a change of a lifestyle, it's a life commitment.

Paul: Yes... So when does this process end?

Heather: It never ends. No, it never ends because if your disease is just crouching at the door, it will be back. If you pick up the alcohol or the drugs again you are not just back where you were. The disease progresses, and so you are further down in the progression. You can never let up your discipline. It becomes easier through the years though. But there are people who have had 20 years recovery and then go out and use again. And they're just miserable. This happens all the time in recovery.

Sometimes that's a deterrent for others to say, "Boy I don't ever want that to happen to me." Maybe some life problem has happened that they are unable to deal with, and they've gone back out again. It's heart breaking. You are never free except when you are working it and surrendered….to God.

Paul: Working it and surrendering it.

Heather: Surrender to God. Yes. That's the only way.

Paul: So, its sounds like these relationships that begin your recovery are with you forever. Different people may be coming and going but the relationship needs ……

Heather: Yes, the need is there. Always. It may be different people. It may be different faces. Often these relationships are tighter than any relationships that you would have anywhere else.

Paul: Why?

Heather: Because these are the relationships where you are not wearing any masks. What you see is what you get. Sometimes out there in the working world you do have to wear a mask, and socially, people wear masks. But in the recovery groups you don't wear that mask because everyone can see through it. They know the mask, they've worn it too. So honesty is there.

I love the church and that's where I've gotten a lot of my healing. It's interesting because my son is very active in NA. We were talking the other day and I said, "You know, there are people who speak against the church because we have failed in many ways. And there are people who speak against recovery because we're imperfect people. I can understand, and I can listen to people say things about the hypocrites in the church, but for me, that was the place that saved my life. I didn't know about recovery then. I only knew that I needed something and I went to the church. I was there day after day. That was my program. Day in and day out, and I surrendered. I did recovery through the church and then later came to know Twelve Step."

If people speak against the church and say "it's not relevant, it's not what we need today," a part of me just grieves inside because it has been so important to me.

I asked my son how he would feel if someone said that to him about Twelve Step. He said that he would just rise up inside, that he would want to defend the program. And I said, "Yes, there is something in you that rises up and says, "Oh, but you don't really know. Yes, they are imperfect people but... they are there."

They are there to try to help you. And I have seen them both. They are so similar, the church and recovery. I have always had a passion for recovery in the church, and I have always been involved in Twelve Step Christian recovery because I enjoy the freedom of being able to call Jesus Christ my higher power. That doesn't mean that I think it's wrong that other people haven't found that place yet. I just like the freedom in a group to be able to share that with other believers who totally understand where I'm coming from.

Paul: Are there some things in the Twelve-Step movement that you would like to see become more common in the church?

Heather: Oh my... Yes. I know that when I came into the church I was an open book because I was hurting so badly. And so I remember sometimes feeling like, "Isn't anybody else crying?""Isn't anybody else saying what they feel?" It seemed like other people had it together but not me. I've heard other people since then that have come in and said the same thing. I want them to know that I was there too. "I was you."

Recovery groups and the church really serve two different purposes. You go to a Twelve Step meeting and you are going to talk about the nitty gritty stuff that really goes on. You go into the church and you are going to talk about the word of God and maybe have some prayer requests but you're not necessarily going to talk about the things that really hurt you. The things that are hard in life. The things that are deep.

That has sometimes been frustrating for me, because I've occasionally had a snoot full of both: the Church and the Twelve Step. It's like I'm ruined. I have to have that openness and honesty. I can't do religion. I can only do relationship and what's real for me.

I'm not saying that it isn't real for other people. I'm just saying that there are times in a church when I've seen a vulnerability in groups and it's really healing and life changing. Those have been wonderful times and that's when there is a move of the Holy Spirit. All the walls are down, and I'm so grateful to be in a church where that happens. That, at any given time the Holy Spirit can just move in our congregation and people's hearts are open, there are no masks, and it's just God. I love those times.

Would I like to see that? I'd like to see that more in the church, yes. And I believe that's by the power of the Spirit. I don't know that you can make that happen. That's God's timing and his calling on people. But I'd like to see more of that.

In everything I'm involved in I try to be vulnerable. I don't have any secrets any more. I spent a lifetime, most of the first part of my life, keeping secrets but I don't have secrets today.

That doesn't always match up with the traditional role of a counselor, because you're taught to keep your boundaries when you're counseling. I do keep boundaries, but people are never just clients to me. I truly care, and I'm not worried about being too vulnerable. I think boundaries can sometimes be walls. I don't want that. I want walls down with people. That's what I want. No walls.

Forbidden Toys

In the beginning we're just little boys, longing to play with forbidden toys,

so bright and shiny they gleamed in the sun, since they were forbidden,

they had to be fun!

The hiding and sneaking would start about then, but one look at us and they

knew where we'd been,

We'd been to the box full of forbidden toys and soon we'd become the lost

Relationship

little boys

What could they have said? What could they have done, to keep us away

from what should have been fun?

My friends no one knows and neither do I, but one thing for sure, many years

have passed by

So now that we're men in the grip of addiction, our chaotic lives full of conflict

and friction,

What will we say to our girls and our boys when they reach for the box full of

forbidden toys?

Written by Gary Larson

1/14/09

PART 3-PRESSING ON:
ONE INTERACTION AT A TIME

I am grateful to be able to call Steve Mason and Dave Browning friends. Though uniquely and dramatically different in personality, style and occasionally viewpoint their individual, long time service to the church is exemplary. I love these guys.

In Chapter 12, I share with you a conversation with Steve Mason, former pastor of Christ the King Community Church, about how care will be provided in the Church if it embraces the concepts we've set forth in this book.

Since his conversion in the 70's, Steve has been a leader in the church and small group movement. Steve literally changed the "spiritual landscape" of Whatcom County, WA, and eventually the world, when in 1989 he became the pastor of what would become Christ the King Community Church in the small town of Laurel, Washington. Over the next 10 years that small, 50 member church grew to over 3,000 people who met in multiple locations and dozens of small groups.

Over the years I'm sure Steve hasn't seen it all, but I think he's seen enough. What I appreciate most about Steve is his deep love for God, His church and its mission to reach the lost with the good news of salvation.

It seems to me that Steve has been "whittled down" over time and that all that is left is an essential love for God and His people and a pure desire to focus only on the the main things.

Relationship

Church-ianity doesn't cut it. Formulas are not readily accepted. "Thoughts du jour" are carefully scrutinized. I love that about him.

As a friend I can always count on Steve to challenge me directly through his comments and indirectly by his behavior. I appreciate that about him as well.

I'm grateful for this opportunity to share one of my moments with Steve. Each of our interactions has been valuable to me and I hope you find the same.

In Chapter 13, Dave Browning, Senior Pastor at Christ the King International, shares his thoughts on where the Church has come from and how it's moving toward being more relational.

Dave Browning's vision, communication skills and work ethic have served the Lord well for probably 20 years or more. As the Senior Pastor of Christ the King International, his impact on both local and international levels is evidence of his commitment to God's kingdom. Though Dave already has a formidable legacy as pastor, author and church planter my suspicion is that the best is yet to come.

Over the years my dialogue with Dave has always helped me to think beyond my comfort zone and to consider multiple perspectives. I may not always be comfortable, but I'm generally invigorated. The most fun times for me are when we innovate, sharing new ideas and "plussing" each other as we co-create. I value our times together.

When it comes to looking out a-ways, trying to "connect the dots" of what God is up to, I always want to hear what Dave has to say. I hope Dave's thoughts impact you as much as they do me.

CHAPTER 12:
HOW WILL CARE BE DELIVERED?

A CONVERSATION WITH
STEVE MASON

Paul: You and I first started working on these concepts and ideas together. As a result I've tried my best to capture the essence of our conversations in writing. We're now working on the third part of the book.

Throughout our meetings you always referred back to a key question that you wanted to be answered. You asked, "How will the church be cared for?" Do you remember?

Steve: "How will care be delivered?"

Paul: "How will care be delivered?" You clearly have insights and thoughts about that subject and I would like to hear them. So, what is that all about, "How will care be delivered?"

Steve: Well, let me ask you a question, so, give me, in three sentences, the content and the theme of this book.

Paul: Okay, part one is laying out the principals of the great commandments. That's really what this whole things all about, living those out one interaction at a time. Part two contains chapters which illustrate how different people have applied these principals in their lives. Part

three addresses how these concepts may impact the church. The original title for this chapter came from you and so here we are.

Steve: Ok, So If it's all about relationships, then the first question is: "Are these relationships going to be spontaneous, or are they going to be structural, are they going to be intentional or does it matter?"

Paul: I would say yes to all and I don't think it matters.

Steve: Ok. So the fundamental question that you and I have been interacting about is, so the church is a structure, inescapably. It has roles, there are responsibilities, whether it's "make sure the chairs are straight on Sunday morning" or that the widows all have enough to eat. There are roles and there are responsibilities and out of those roles and responsibilities automatically there are going to be relationships.

Do we just let life happen and as it happens, we love God with all of our heart, mind, strength, soul, love our neighbor as ourself or, within the framework of the church, that structure, is there an intentional effort or direction or mandate or command that care should flow from those who have it to those who need it? And if that's true, how does, in the traditional church, how does care get delivered? So, how do you think care gets delivered in the traditional church?

Paul: Badly.

Steve: Ok. Why?

Paul: Because it's top down, its staff driven, I think the church doesn't always act like the church. I think many don't understand any longer what it means for them to be part of the church, what is expected of them. I think they've placed their expectations on a handful of leaders or

pastors and they have become "the audience" when they were always intended to be the actors.

Steve: Ok. So that's a pretty broad brush they and them and everybody but.....

Paul: Yes, but you asked about the church.

Steve: That's broad. Yes, exactly, but so then you've just defined the problem. So if that's the problem, we have some choices in terms of how we respond to it. Do we do more of the same or will we begin to ask the question, "How in this church, will care be delivered?"

I think the thesis of your material here is that everybody's empowered to deliver care. That's in the unfolding of life as life events come and so on. You come across a need, you're responsible to meet it. So it would be a really awesome church where the pastor could say: "you're all empowered" and everybody lived in that empowerment and everybody went and did it. Think that's going to happen?

Paul: I think the degree to which it does happen will be... will tell the whole story of the church on earth.

Steve: That strikes at the very crux of the mission of your book. I mean that's right at the core of this issue. Because if I understand it, if we were to embrace the paradigm that you are proposing, then the answer, "Do I think that's going to happen?", would be "absolutely". Because you are all empowered. "Here's how we're going to deliver care. We're going to love God with all our hearts and were going to love each other. With this Christ centered, spirit filled, unselfish expression of the Holy Spirit flowing through us, we're going to love each other. We're going to do it in every exchange and you're all empowered to go and do it." That's what we're proposing here.

Paul: Yes.

Steve: So on one hand, that answers the question in this church. "How will care be delivered?" Well, everybody is going to do it. Now, I don't see that necessarily working well within the structure or the current paradigm. So, are you a paradigm changer? Is that what we're working on here?

Paul: I think, first of all, I want to go back to that question, "Will that happen?" I think that it's prophesied that it will. But It's a matter of choice. People of God have got to choose this. I'm trying to make a case. I'm trying to take something that's older than the hills and bring it back up to the surface for people to make a choice. I can't control their choice. The Holy Spirit is the great convincer of our soul. I can't convince you of anything. Nothing. Ok? So, I'm not going to burn up a lot of energy on that so..... will that happen? Yes I think it will. If I look at the end story, yes, it's going to happen. This book, what's the purpose of it? I think it's to say, "Here is the case, you've got a choice to make." And if that changes paradigms, well, I don't see the current paradigm in the bible.

Steve: Right, right.

Paul: Why do we hold on so tightly to it? I don't know why. It's one of a billion other possible paradigms. There's certainly nothing sacred about it. So, I'm not taking responsibility for that. It's hard enough for me to hold onto the simplicity... to just do it myself. This all means nothing if I don't.

Steve: Well we hold on to the paradigm because it's the one we have. That's the only reason why we hold on to it is because it's the one we have. And until we can have eyes to see a different one we can't let go of the one we have.

So the question is, and you and I talked about this at length but, if we were initiating this for the first time and you were talking to me about the church, then I would press in on you and I would say, "Ok, Paul, but how will care be delivered?" And you'd say, "Well, we have a pastor." And I'd say, "But how will care be delivered?" And I'd just stay on that until hopefully we began to see that in our current context the level of care that we're delivering is really pretty thin.

Now if I'm in that inner circle in the church, relationally, and I'm in the hospital, and my pastor knows me well and he knows my family, he's been in my home and my family is all gathered at the hospital, there's a high level of care at a personal level from that pastor…there is a high probability that at a personal level from that pastor that I'm going to receive incredible care.

So is that pastor a caring person? Does he give genuine care, does he give quality care? The answer could very well be, "absolutely." However, how many people can a person like that care for? Particularly where he knows me, he knows my kids, he knows my grandkids, he's been in my home because I'm on the church council or I'm the head Deacon or I'm the adult Sunday school teacher or I'm the treasurer. But does he know that guy that's been sitting in the third row from the back for the last six months who doesn't talk to anybody? Does he know him that well? And would that guy get that level of care? Chances are probably not. Simply because, as you stated, this all comes down to relationships. So how will care be delivered?

Well, perhaps at some point, the strategists in the church need to look through a biblical lens and figure out, in harmony with scripture, are there structures that we can put in place that, out of those intentional structures, relationships will come?

So now we're in to small groups. Small groups are not about what you study and it's not about what video you watch. Small groups are not about any of that. Small groups are about building relationships. They're about learning to love one another, serve one another, care for one another, obey all the other commands of Jesus. What other contexts can we explore?

Paul: I don't think that's clear though, by the way.

Steve: No, but you know what? I've been preaching that and teaching that for 25 years and it's not clear. I've held seminars for hundreds of pastors. I couldn't get my own staff to understand that. But I'll tell you what, there are still small groups in Whatcom county [Washington State] that are still going. They're under the radar. Nobody cares for them. Nobody supports them. You couldn't kill them to save your life because they get it. And I run into these people and they say, "You know we still have our small group". I run into them all the time. "Nobody from the church has called me in four years but we still got our small group". Because it's about relationships.

So, that's really the question, "How will care be delivered?" So we're really talking about a paradigm. I mean to use the popular language we are talking about a paradigm shift and you know Covey says that if you want to make small changes, work on attitudes and disciplines and whatever, whatever, whatever but if you really want to change something, change the paradigm.

And you know, there was a doctor named Semmelweis in the 1800's who started washing his hands whenever he delivered babies. He had a different paradigm. Germ theory, which the other doctors didn't have. They didn't get it because they were stuck here and then he discovered it and then it took years and years for it to eventually catch on and change. Maybe this is one of those scenarios where it's going to take.....I mean at some point do we find the church doors locked, a government official standing outside saying, the property has been repossessed or whatever or until.....

Paul: It wouldn't hurt the church.

Steve: It wouldn't. It would revitalize the church because it would push us from this current structure.

Paul: You know what I think Steve? I think you and I both lived through the Jesus movement.

Steve: Yes.

Paul: Nobody wrote down that paradigm, described it, made a strategic plan, had goals. When the Spirit moved, it moved. And a lot of what we have now, the paradigm, if you want to call it that, is a pretty poor attempt to imitate what happened back then but without the power, without the... you know, it has some form but... and I believe that it kind of happened one person at a time. I got saved in the bedroom, I didn't get saved in a church,

Steve: Me too, me too.

Paul: And I didn't know the difference.

Steve: I didn't go to church.

Paul: Oh, am I supposed to be in church?

Steve: I didn't go to church until after I got born again, thoroughly born again. That's right.

Paul: So, look, you know, I believe that's the way it's going to be.

Steve: So that raises a question though. That was the wind of the Spirit that captured us and we would long to see that again. But we can't create it. If you are a follower of Charles Finney then you are of the conviction that when we get right enough with God and we pray long enough with God that then, and only then, will revival happen. But that's Finney's perspective, you know. But you go over here to Packer and his followers and they just say, flat out say, "You know what? There will be revival when God wants revival. Nothing you ever do is going to change that." So, who knows?

But, we are where we are, and the church that we have still belongs to Jesus and he loves it. And as screwed up as it is, he died for it. And, he's at work in it. So, in to that then, how can this material be presented as an invitation? I mean, "draw near to me, and I will draw near to you." So how can there be a new prophetic voice that simply says, you know, "the master cometh and he calleth for thee", and out of that then, this intimate relationship with the lord, that manifests itself and this one another kind of love? But how can we challenge or invite, those who are....if you saw somebody in a burning building and you could holler at them and get them out, you'd do it.

Paul: Yes.

Steve: If you saw somebody drowning in a swimming pool and you could throw them a rope, you would do it. Well if we're stuck in a church structure that deludes us into to thinking that it's the pastor's job to deliver care and robs the people who could be delivering the care from the joy and the fulfillment of living up to their potential in Christ, we will throw them a life line.

So, that simply comes back to the question, you know. I think we're confronted with the question to the existing structure, the existing church. You know, "How will care be delivered in your congregation?" I don't think there is a profound answer to that and I don't think there's a right way or a wrong way other than anything that you do that creates relationships heightens the probability that somebody is going to love somebody in their moment of need. I don't know.

Paul: Yes, I have never actually have thought about this in terms of the church structure discussion.

Steve: If you take the church structure out of it, the question, "How will care be delivered?" really was a question for the church. That's the question. "How will care be delivered?" It's a question for every pastor up and down the street here. If it's general question then you've answered the question, "How will care be delivered?" It's going to be delivered out of these one another relationships. Therein lies the answer.

Paul: I think though... Here's the state of the church, more people do not attend a church service on Sunday... believers... than do. Ok?

Steve: Correct.

Paul: Are they part of the church?

Steve: Absolutely.

Paul: So we've got this "us and them" thing. Low and behold there are all kinds of interesting things going on and we are unaware. Now, these are my brothers and sisters. Many of them are past leaders. Those are the most dissatisfied people with this current paradigm of all.

Steve: Right.

Paul: But if we're going to change, if we're going to move the church, we've got to acknowledge the state of the church today.

Steve: Right.

Relationship

Paul: So now, when you talk about the confines of a wall, that's only one part.

Steve: Right.

Paul: So you have to find a solution that goes beyond walls and hierarchies or charts, strategic plans, paradigms, and ...

Steve: Well.... you are exactly right. You can do quadrant theory and divide this up. You've got the non-churched Christian and you have the churched Christian and the non-Christian. It's probably long now forgotten because things have moved on but the whole initial ministry around Christ the King [Church], was targeted specifically at non-Christians and non-churched Christians. That was the deal.

We used to tell people, "Hey, If you're a Christian, and you are already going to a church, unless you want to work your butt off don't come here." You know? And I had whole rows of people get up and walk out. I'd say something like, "This is not a church for the already saved. Get back to where you came from. We don't want you." Then they would get up and walk out and they would be mad.

So no, I couldn't agree more. That's... see I'm driven by the idea that people really need to be connected. The branch and the vine and the fruit and the gardener are all part of the story. And I believe you when you tell me, "I am a Christian and I pray every day and I love god and I know Jesus saved me but I don't go to church." What I want to know is who are you connected with? "Well, I watch Joyce Myers." Well bless your heart, you know. And I'm glad that that feeds your soul and that encourages you but I want to know who you are connected with and, basically, when I ask the question who are you connecting with and how is care delivered? Those are the same questions, Paul, just at different levels.

Paul: That's right.

Steve: And the existing church with all of its warts cannot escape the scrutiny and the responsibility that they are a part of this equation and we have these dissatisfied people out there because they were looking for a level of spiritual satisfaction in a structure. You can't get it from a structure, you can only get it from relationships. So we can't just throw the churches out... we're all in this together.

But it's like this thing with spiritual gifts. We promised people they were going to learn their gifts and that they were going to have a meaningful ministry. The only exciting part of that equation was the first two nights you went to class when you thought you were going to learn something about yourself you didn't know before. From there on out it was all downhill.

Paul: Yes.

Steve: You know, it was incredibly disappointing and heartbreaking. You go to yard sales and you find these spiritual gifts books laying around, three quarters of the way filled out and .... because we promised what we couldn't deliver because spiritual gifts won't satisfy your soul unless they function in some kind of context that's relational.

And being in a small group is not an automatic answer. Peter Wagner had an adult Sunday school class of about 90 people in Fall Cedars Church in Pasadena and I don't even remember what kind of church it was. But he had a church within the church. And I mean they cared for the sick, they prayed for the sick, they delivered meals, they had Koinonia, they shopped together, they tripped together, I mean they had fellowship, which was a big thing by the way, in the 70's. Which you don't hear. When was the last time you heard a sermon on fellowship? Think about that.

Paul: Boy ...

Steve: I'm thinking about it right now. Think about that but, Koinonia, that was one of the big words, Koinonia. But they had a structure and this was probably a leadership thing, creating those relationships. Yet I could take you to adult class after adult class where there is one guy studying all week long to talk for 45 to 50 minutes and everybody else just sitting there listening and being unconnected. So the structure.... it's not the structure that provokes the relationship but there's got...but there's something within the structure that can. So, who are you connected to and how will care be delivered? I mean, they are basically the same question. I think that's the question. I mean, the church isn't going away.

Paul: Right.

Steve: And for all of its......

Paul: When you say the church ...

Steve: I'm talking about the visible structure, the organized, weak, anemic, dysfunctional, ingrown, hypocritical church. It isn't going away and, regardless of what our critics think, God's at work even there. Now he's not at work only there but he's at work.

There's only one church but we can say we are talking about two expressions in the church. The publicly organized, attended, definable, visible structure on the corner of first and main and the church of the un-churched which is out in their homes and communities and so on. So, you can ask the same question to both groups. "How is care delivered?"

Paul: Right. I agree.

Steve: Over here, "How is care delivered?" Over here, "Who are you connected to?" Just because you've got a chair you sit in every Sunday morning doesn't mean you're connected to anybody. Who are you connected to? So, if there's a question that can be asked then our assumption is there's an answer that can be given. And maybe the answer here is different than the answer over there. Or maybe the answer is the same for everybody. And maybe it's as simple as "love God with all your heart, and love your neighbor as yourself."

Paul: Yes. I've been feeling some real angst about this division in the church.

Steve: Oh, nobody wins. Nobody wins.

Paul: Oh, the enemy wins.

Steve: Well, yes, maybe but yes.

Paul: Short term. But I don't think there is any difference between the two groups. Now, the people who can't say that, I think, are the ones who might have a problem. The fact is a believer is a believer and a connection is a connection.

Steve: Absolutely.

Paul: The form of method or methodology is irrelevant as long as the proper result is achieved.

Steve: Absolutely.

Paul: I went to a Catholic funeral a couple of months ago. They were saying some good stuff.

Steve: Oh I love the Catholics. That's why Christ the King is a Catholic name, because I grew up in a Catholic neighborhood.

Paul: Oh wow.

Steve: That's where that came from.

Paul: Really?

Steve: Our family was the only family on the block that wasn't Catholic. I love the Catholics. I'd be a Catholic if I could believe in transubstantiation. I would be a Catholic, I love the Catholics. I love their reverence for God.

Paul: Yes.

Steve:(looking at his computer) Oh Lord, help me find this right now. Ok, here we go... now this is old. This goes back to March. Ok, "Our mission is to love God with all our hearts, our souls, or minds and all our strength, love our neighbors as ourselves. Our mission in church reaches out to people who are in spiritual poverty and invites them to become fully devoted followers of Christ. Our task is freeing people who are held captive by the god of this age. And equip people for life and ministry."

Ok, here it is. Here's the deal, now you're getting my bias, that's all you're getting. But here is what I believe is the task at hand. So who's our target group? Christians who have given up on church, those who have never belonged, those who have been wounded in service and those who long for a purpose worth spending their lives for. Our target is the people who are either outside of or are not comfortable with the circle of the status quo.

They are the visionaries on the fringes. They are the believers who long for something they can spend their lives for. If it's not real, they are not interested. They cannot be convinced or fooled. They want to participate in real ministry and they know it when they find it.

See that's…this is what's in front of us right now. So, if you ask me, Pastor Steve, "How will care be delivered?" It's by living out with authenticity this simple command of Jesus with an eye, an eye toward reconnecting with these people. Because every one of these…and here's the tension, Paul, for me, and I'm going to use a word, two words, "displaced" and "unfranchised" or "non-franchised". Because I'm not sure whether we need to get the people from this structure over here with this group or whether we need to get this group over here with this group. Or, whether we need to get both groups someplace else… someplace new.

Paul: I would give you a fourth option, which is… let them continue as they are going but get the right priorities in place. When you said that…well if you said it to the average church staff or pastor, "Do you know that the number one reason for your existence is to see that care is delivered to the church? Do you know that? Is that your primary goal? Is that how you make decisions?"

Steve: Absolutely not. I make decisions, Paul, based upon the survival of the church, the structure of the budget and whether I get paid or not.

Paul: It's the only way it's going to become the light of the world.

Steve: Right.

Paul: So, that's how essentially important this message is to me and that's why it's worth giving my life for.

Steve: Exactly, there you go. That's why you are passionate about it.

Relationship

Paul: Ok, because you see, there's no way the church will be healthy without each individual... using their individual gifts and building that relationship in such a way that it spills over to those around them.

Steve: Do you go to church most Sundays?

Paul: I've been going to ---------- recently.

Steve: Why do you go?

Paul: Mostly because I want to see what God is up to... I like seeing people.

Steve: No, no, no, no, I just wanted you to say that.

Paul: Oh. I want to see what God's up to.

Steve: Because God is up to something.

Paul: I actually have a sense of optimism, that the lord has allowed the church this permution and it is not unhealthy. I think It's all part of what's supposed to happen.

Steve: See, I'm telling people, don't despair. This is the greatest moment in my life time to return to an authentic expression of Christianity, Paul. I believe it. Don't despair over the general. This is what I'm telling people. I said, don't despair over the state of the nation. Don't despair over the general state of the church. The darker the night, I'll tell you when God moves...

Paul: It's happening.

Steve: Yes.

Paul: And it's going to happen.

Steve: Yes. I couldn't be more optimistic.

Paul: Me too.

Steve: Yes. Absolutely, absolutely.

Paul: The words that are resonating for me right now are reconciliation, acceptance, love, hope. I'm really not interested in being right or wrong. If you tell me I'm wrong, I'm ok with that.

Steve: Well, you can be wrong because we are freely justified and, seriously, that's the beauty of it. That's the deal. It's all good news, it's all good news. But whether the question is being asked formally, or informally, whether it's being asked of an individual, or an organized group of individuals, the question still exists, "How will care be delivered?"

Paul: That ' s true.

Steve: Who are you connected to? And you know…what is your personal part in all of this?

Paul: That's the key.

Steve: Because we…we teach what we do not do, I mean that's the deal. It's all so bogus till you do it.

Paul: I ' m doing it.

Steve: Awesome.

Relationship

Paul: I'm not very good at it, but I'm doing it. I get better sometimes and I screw it up sometimes. Doesn't matter to the Lord. He just wants me to keep practicing at it. Even what I think are mistakes, are probably something that the Holy Spirit is going to use somehow.

Steve: Well, you know what? We're trying. We've got a brain the size of a Big Gulp from 711. We are trying to understand a God that is without measure.

I might have told you this before, but I've got a glimpse of just how deep the ocean of God's love is and It's amazing. I've got a fresh new glimpse of the immeasurable depths of God's love and God's goodness and God's favor and how our small, linear, humanistic view of the world around us....we just don't get it. It's interesting. I can't really talk about this because I can't really articulate it well but... and maybe I'm getting old... but I'm seeing now in the writings of other people like Andrew Murray and Ian Bounds and more current guys and ancient guys like Martin Luther... I'm seeing little bits and pieces of a resonating revelation. It's like either they couldn't articulate with clarity or they just have little fragments of the puzzle. But they all match. It's fascinating. Absolutely fascinating.

Paul: That's what Paul was talking about "in the mirror dimly."

Steve: That's right. That is right.

Paul: That's all you've got to work with.

Steve: That's right. Well, I believe that, Paul. I believe the wind of revival is blowing... And you can... you raise your sail and you are going to catch it or you are not. The real signature of the Spirit of God. I believe, and this is just my perspective, but I believe the real signature of the Holy Spirit and this coming revival is that we are going to start seeing people get saved. I mean... I believe it.

I told somebody the other day. I said, "I don't know why, I don't know how, I don't when, but I know it. It's just a matter of time until our church is full of college students again." I just know it. I just know it and I don't know why I know it, but I know it.

Paul: Yes.

Steve: You know.

Paul: Yes, I do. I have that sense too.

CHAPTER 13:
THE RELATIONAL CHURCH

BY DAVE BROWNING

Sheri Drew says, "These are the days in which a true leader wants to live. These are days when opportunities to change lives and even destinies are nearly endless. You are running the anchor leg of the relay because you were born to lead. You were born for glory."

Certainly, for Christian leaders entering the third millennium these words ring true. Now is the time for the church to fulfill its destiny. But first the church must undergo a second time of reformation. Only this time it will be of a reformation of behavior, instead of belief.

Throughout history, churches have delivered three things in some combination: Information, Experiences and Relationships (every church delivers all these three in some combination and sequence.)

The Informational Church

Throughout much of church history the church has had a primary emphasis on information, secondarily on experiences and relationships. This was because for most of church history believers did not have a copy of the scripture in their own hands. Prior to the invention of the printing press, priests and pastors were clearly needed to read, translate and explain the scriptures to the masses. It was necessary to attend the parish, so that the priest or minister could explain the scriptures. The local minister was often the most learned individual in the community. The church was center of education and literacy.

With the dawn of the information age, the church has gone through a time of significant change. With mass media and the digital explosion, people no longer need to come to church to get the Information they need. There are much more efficient ways to gain knowledge than attending a thirty minute lecture (sermon) every week, hoping that the pastor eventually answers your questions. It is much more efficient to "Google" any question or passage of scripture and you will be treated to a wealth of sermons and articles at your fingertips. It's not that the church no longer delivers information. It's just that this cannot be the only thing it delivers (unless, that is, you want to die a slow and painful death).

The Experiential Church

Moving away from information as a primary suit, the church has found a couple ways it can go to add value: toward Experiences or toward Relationships. The direction popularized in the past few decades has been toward Experiences. I would dare say that 95% of the growing churches in America today have gone this route. Why? Because of the influence of Willow Creek Community Church in Chicago. In the 1980s, as many denominational churches were slipping in attendance, Willow Creek burst onto the scene with a band, actors and video projection. The church service was no longer a dull, boring "information dump." It was a moving experience that you wanted to bring your friends to...well...to experience.

In the past 25 years thousands of church leaders have made their pilgrimage to Willow Creek and been inspired to incorporate the arts into their "experience." Many churches have experienced good results from what they've been able to glean from Willow. Some churches have even begun calling their weekend services "Weekend Experiences." This is an appropriate description considering the shift from the primacy of Information to the primacy of Experience. Not all "Experience Churches" are the same, however. As time has gone on, the Experience path has branched off in four directions:

1. Experience Our Pastor

For some churches, the "experience" is located in the dynamism of the pastor. There are many churches across America that are now built on the dynamism and charisma of the teacher. When the Experience is about the pastor you might hear people say, "You've got to come and experience our pastor." As an example of this kind of Experience Church I would hold up Mars Hill Church in Seattle. Mark Driscoll, the pastor, is a bright, articulate, sometimes controversial communicator. Listening to Mark preach is an experience. He says some very interesting things in a very interesting way. You may not agree with everything he stands for, but at least he stands for something. I know that some people feel that Mars Hills' growth is a result of its candle-burning vibe (a young, artsy, urban culture), but I respectfully disagree. I believe its growth is a reflection of Mark's vibe. The greatest evidence that I'm right is that Mars Hill projects Mark's teaching at all of its campuses. He is the draw. Mark is the show.

2. Experience Our Programs

When the experience is about the programming you might hear people say, "You won't believe everything we have going on." As an example of this kind of Experience church I would suggest Saddleback Church in Southern California. Rick Warren is their well-known pastor, but not because he is a such a compelling speaker. It is because Saddleback has put together such a compelling program. Some of their programs are so good, in fact, that they have become industries of their own (40 Days of Purpose, Celebrate Recovery, etc.). When I went on a behind the scenes tour of Saddleback a few years ago I was struck by how excited my guide was about the programs that were happening there. Rick's gifts are many, to be sure, but the one that has created the greatest waves is administration. Yes, they have great teaching and worship, but the programs are the show.

3. Experience Our Passion

When the Experience is about the passion you might hear someone say, "You need to experience our worship." As an example of this kind of Experience church I would mention Hillsong Church in Australia. In the case of Hillsong, I actually don't know the pastor's name. But their worship leaders are world-renowned. Their worship experience is unbelievable. Powerful. Worth telling others about. So now leaders are making their pilgrimage to Australia in hopes of importing this passionate worship dynamic to the U.S. In one American location where this model is being replicated they have actually called the ministry "Passion." Yes, they have a dynamic teacher, but to a greater extent, the worship is the Experience.

4. Experience Our Production

When the experience is about the production you might hear someone say, "You will be blown away by our service." As an example of this kind of Experience church I would reference LifeChurch.tv. LifeChurch presents a very potent cocktail of music, video and teaching via satellite to a number of locations. LifeChurch has been recognized as the most innovative church in America. I have visited their campuses near Oklahoma City and become friends with some of their production team. They truly are bringing a level of creativity that is astounding. Yes, the elements are cool in and of themselves, but it's how it's all put together that is the Experience.

I believe that the attractional/experiential paradigm has almost been "wrung out." I say that because of Lakewood Church in Houston, Texas, the largest church in America. It is clearly an Experience church, and I would say that it is an amalgamation of the four varieties of Experience church. They have put together in one place the Pastor experience (Joel Osteen is a true celebrity), the Program experience (a huge facility that houses a multitude of ministries), the Passion experience (a worship experience that is as powerful as any), and the Production experience (Joel was actually the producer of the television program prior to becoming pastor). In my way of thinking it is the ultimate expression of this paradigm. Where do we go from here? What's next? What's left? The Relational church.

The Relational Church

Another possibility is to see the church have a primary emphasis on Relationships. I call this "the road less travelled." I believe that the path from Information to Experiences is so well-worn that many have not even considered the existence of "another way to go," toward the primacy of relationships. This was the modus operandi of the early (first century) church. And I believe that the church of the future is going to look like the church of the past, with a primary emphasis on relationships.

At CTK, we deliver Relationships (or at least attempt to do so). We have a saying that "Small groups are our plan A and we don't have a plan B." Why are we so high on Relationships? First, because Relationships are simple. You do not need a production crew, or special lighting. You do not need a budget. You do not need advance planning – you can start right away. All you need is love. Second, because Relationships are satisfying. Something rings hollow about the Experience church after awhile. It's like eating your favorite dessert day after day…lots of calories, but not a lot of nutrition. Is there something more that I'm missing? And third, because Relationships are scalable. We can go as far as relationships will take us. And we're finding that is pretty far. The CTK story now consists of friendships, groups and gatherings all around the world.

The Two Great Commandments

The church of the first century was an organic, relational movement. In the book of Acts, we find the first-century church meeting in homes and gathering in public spaces for assembly. The early church was not about religion but relationships.... loving God with all your heart, soul, mind and strength, and loving your neighbor as yourself. It was that simple. In a relational church, relationships are the end, the means and the mission. Jesus said that relationships are the goal.

Mark 12:28-34

One of the teachers of the law came and heard them debating. Noticing that Jesus had given them a good answer, he asked him, "Of all the commandments, which is the most important?" "The most important one," answered Jesus, "is this: 'Hear, O Israel, the Lord our God, the Lord is one. Love the Lord your God with all your heart and with all your soul and with all your mind and with all your strength.' The second is this: 'Love your neighbor as yourself.' There is no commandment greater than these."

"Well said, teacher," the man replied. "You are right in saying that God is one and there is no other but him. To love him with all your heart, with all your understanding and with all your strength, and to love your neighbor as yourself is more important than all burnt offerings and sacrifices." When Jesus saw that he had answered wisely, he said to him, "You are not far from the kingdom of God." And from then on no one dared ask him any more questions.

Relationship

I think here we see the genius of Jesus on full display. One of the reasons I believe in Jesus is that I believe that Jesus was the smartest man who ever lived I believe he had the best information possible on the most important topics in life. Here, Jesus answered this man's question in an amazing way, both in what he answered and how he answered. The questioner asked, "What's the one, greatest commandment?" We know from other accounts that he was trying to paint Jesus into a corner. But Jesus is too smart for that. He doesn't take the bait. He answers with a wisdom that is uncanny. He says, "It's about love" – and love that is in two directions: For God…For people. He was asked for one. He comes back with two (though they begin with the save verb): Love God and love your neighbor. He says treat God the way he'd like to be treated, and treat people the way you'd like to be treated. Why did Jesus give two commandments instead of one:

1. Because the two rise above the others.

When Jesus was asked about the Great Commandment, His reply made clear that two actually stood out above the rest.

Mark 12:30,31

Love the Lord your God with all your heart and with all your soul and with all your mind and with all your strength. The second is this: Love your neighbor as yourself. There is no commandment greater than these."

Jesus indicated that the two separate themselves from the rest of the pack. They are to the commandments what Magic Johnson and Larry Bird were to professional basketball. Evidently no other commands approximate loving God and loving your neighbor in stature.

2. Because these two are the key to all the others.

In Matthew's account of this interaction, he describes the two commands as linchpins for the other commands.

Matthew 22:36-40

"Teacher, which is the greatest commandment in the Law?" Jesus replied: "'Love the Lord your God with all your heart and with all your soul and with all your mind.' This is the first and greatest commandment. And the second is like it: 'Love your neighbor as yourself.' All the Law and the Prophets hang on these two commandments."

Evidently, if we love God the way we should, and love our neighbor the way we should, the other commands will automatically be fulfilled. You can see this in specificity when you take another look at the Ten Commandments. Each of the commands will automatically be fulfilled if we are sufficiently loving toward God and people.

1. No other Gods. (God)

2. No idols. (God)

3. Don't misuse God's name. (God)

4. Remember the Sabbath. (God)

5. Honor your father and mother. (Neighbor)

6. Don't murder. (Neighbor)

7. Don't commit adultery. (Neighbor)

8. Don't steal. (Neighbor)

9. Don't lie. (Neighbor)

10. Don't covet. (Neighbor)

If we love God the way we should, we will have Him in the place where he belongs, honoring his name as we should, and giving Him the time He deserves. If we love our neighbor, we will not dishonor, murder, cheat, steal, lie or covet.

Interestingly, when Jesus came he did not talk very much about the Ten Commandments. Instead, He spoke to the deficiency that is underneath our sin - a lack of love. So Jesus did not tell us to sin less. He told us to love more. If we love like we need to love, we will live like we need to live.

3. Because we can't do one without the other.

Jesus said the second command is "like" the first one; meaning corresponding to the first one. These two go together like salt and pepper, peanut butter and jelly, ketchup and mustard, fish and chips, spaghetti and meatballs, arsenic and old lace, Batman and Robin, Bogey and Bacall, Romeo and Juliet, Dick and Jane, Jack and Jill, Mickie and Minnie, Frick and Frack, Mutt and Jeff, Puss and Boots, Lucy and Desi, Hall and Oates, Sonny and Cher, Brooks and Dunn, Yogi and Booboo, Bullwinkle and Rocky, Gilligan and the Skipper...I think you get my (Jesus') point.

Matthew 22:37-39

Love the Lord your God with all your heart and with all your soul and with all your mind. This is the first and greatest commandment. And the second is like it: Love your neighbor as yourself.

You can't love God the way you want to love God, unless you love people. You can't love people the way you want to love people, unless you love God.

4. Because they balance each other.

Jesus indicated in his answer that there is both a vertical and horizontal aspect to Christianity.

Mark 12:30,31

Love the Lord your God...Love your neighbor.

The reason I am not in a monastery right now, is because Jesus gave two great commands, not one. I see some believers who are so heavenly minded that they are of no earthly good. They are super spiritual, super studious, super transcendent. They show God a lot of love...and show very little love for their neighbor. This is not what Jesus is looking for. He is looking for balance.

On the other hand, some are totally into humanitarian efforts. They are volunteering. They are taking care of people. They are serving. And God can somehow get lost in all of that. Service for God can be the greatest enemy of devotion to him. It's both/and not either/or. What God is after is both...in balance.

5. Because narrowing it down simplifies the Christian experience.

In some contexts you get the feeling that Christianity is almost too complicated and confusing for the common person to understand. Do you have to be a Greek scholar, a historian with a Ph.D, or a learned theologian to follow Christ? Not at all. If you want to be a God-follower, the key word to remember is love.

Relationship

You see an expansion and explanation of this in Luke's account of the great commandment.

Luke 10:25-37

On one occasion an expert in the law stood up to test Jesus. "Teacher," he asked, "what must I do to inherit eternal life?" "What is written in the Law?" he replied. "How do you read it?" He answered: "'Love the Lord your God with all your heart and with all your soul and with all your strength and with all your mind'; and, 'Love your neighbor as yourself.'" "You have answered correctly," Jesus replied. "Do this and you will live."

But he wanted to justify himself, so he asked Jesus, "And who is my neighbor?" In reply Jesus said: "A man was going down from Jerusalem to Jericho, when he fell into the hands of robbers. They stripped him of his clothes, beat him and went away, leaving him half dead. A priest happened to be going down the same road, and when he saw the man, he passed by on the other side. So too, a Levite, when he came to the place and saw him, passed by on the other side.

But a Samaritan, as he traveled, came where the man was; and when he saw him, he took pity on him. He went to him and bandaged his wounds, pouring on oil and wine. Then he put the man on his own donkey, took him to an inn and took care of him. The next day he took out two silver coins and gave them to the innkeeper. 'Look after him,' he said, 'and when I return, I will reimburse you for any extra expense you may have.'

"Which of these three do you think was a neighbor to the man who fell into the hands of robbers?" The expert in the law replied, "The one who had mercy on him." Jesus told him, "Go and do likewise."

Jesus' answer to "Who is my neighbor" is clear. Your neighbor is anyone with whom you come in contact, who has a need, that you can meet. This means that as followers of God we need to simply get good at loving, tending to our relationships, and being a blessing. As Peter Block opines, "The shift we seek needs to be embodied in each invitation we make, each relationship we encounter, and each meeting we attend. For at the most operational and practical level, after all the thinking about policy, strategy, mission and milestones, it gets down to this: how are we going to be when we gather together?"

Blessings of the Relational Church

As impacting as the Informational Church or Experiential Church has been, the Relational Church has the most potential to reach the world for Christ. For one, the Relational Church is amazingly cost-effective. It doesn't cost you any money to begin a relationship with someone. It does, however, cost you time. Which ends up being one of the reasons the Informational and Experiential Church cannot afford it. They have all of their time invested in programming. There is little time left for face-to-face community.

My daughter Jenna found out just how important time is to relationships at her place of work. She is a waitress in a restaurant. There are different sections in the restaurant. The more experienced waitresses get the sections with the most tables. One night she was assigned the busiest section, and expected that she would earn the most tips. But when she came home, I could tell she was disappointed. When I asked her what accounted for the lower tips her reply was prescient, "I was so busy that I didn't get to spend as much time with each table." There's an analogy for life and ministry there. It's the quality, not the quantity of relationships that matter.

And for those who appreciate Information and Experiences, I have good news. Relationships, in addition to being winsome in their own right, end up being a great carrier for Information and Experiences. While you can certainly glean the essence of Christianity by hearing someone give a presentation about it, you can also watch someone live it. This seemed to be Jesus' primary approach: "Follow me, and I will make you fishers of men." He taught his disciples many things, but from the context of relationships. They did life together, so the disciples saw what He was talking about, lived out. This is the best combination possible.

Relationships also end up being the best carrier for Experiences. While it is a great experience to be in a large auditorium of people who are engaged in a presentation, it is also a compelling experience to sit with one person, and share deeply about your faith, frustrations and fears. In fact, the experiences that have had the most long-lasting effect on me occurred in a small group, not a crowd. By the church choosing to lead with Relationships, the church ends up touching all the bases, delivering Information and Experiences, as well.

AFTERTHOUGHT: BEING LOVED

The other day a friend of mine called to invite me to a movie. We negotiated movie titles and show times and arrived on a mutually agreeable decision. No big deal.

Upon hanging up I was struck by the nature of that interaction. It was awkward for both of us and I began to wonder why. My friend, who is not a socialable person by nature, was offering me an opportunity to share a movie together, partially because he wanted to see the movie but partially because he cared about me. And I realized that the awkwardness was because of my difficulty in accepting even a simple gesture of affection.

As a result of this interaction I began to reflect on a pattern of behavior in my life that I'd never before comprehended. Receiving a compliment has always made me uncomfortable. Accepting birthday and Christmas gifts is difficult. Giving, for me, is joyful. Receiving is a challenge.

I know that others love me but it literally pains me to accept their expressions of love for me. Similarly, I know God loves me but I now realize that I have not come remotely close to appropriating the fullness of His love or the love of others for me.

It is humbling to death. It is out of my control and therefore I am suspicious of it. I am in control of what I give but I cannot control the love of others for me. I must only accept it.

Relationship

My conclusion is that our efforts to love God and others, though they are essential to living a healthy life, are sadly insignifcant compared to our willingness and ability to be loved.

Being loved may very well be the most powerful, life-changing thing we will ever have. We can't "do it." We can't earn it. We don't deserve it.

Beloved. It's an old fashioned and seldom used word. It may, however, be the key to everything. Beloved. Be loved. Go ahead, be loved!

This is love: not that we loved God, but that he loved us and sent his Son as an atoning sacrifice for our sins. 1 John 4:10

Paul

ACKNOWLEDGEMENTS

I'd like to thank God, first of all, for the great gift of life. For the many, many times He's corrected my course (sometimes painfully), for always loving me, for helping me to know that I am never alone. I hope that His light shines through me to others every day I am on this planet and that every day I can do my best to get the heck out of His way!

The greatest gift He's given me is my husband, Jim, who is my constant supporter, best friend, and love of my life. Without his financial and moral support, it would be much more difficult to share my talents with the world and I am blessed to be his wife.

My kids, Brad and AJ, have been a humble reminder that life is not within my control. They have provided the ultimate lesson in change, in growing, in learning. They have taught me that life isn't perfect, I am not perfect, and I need to release perfection. I wouldn't trade being their mom for the world and I am so proud of the people they are and are becoming.

Finally, I am forever grateful for Paul Evanson and the gift he and his family have been in my life. When I met Paul when we were working at Starbucks Corporate Offices over 20 years ago (!), I had no idea that God was giving me a friend and mentor that would last a lifetime. Because of Paul, I've had a fruitful consulting career that also enabled me to be here for my kids. His love and guidance, along with that of his wife, Jean, and daughter, Megan, have made a tremendous difference in how I've lived my life and who I am as a human being in this world.

It has been an honor to share the journey of this book with such a talented and special friend. Thank you, Paul, for all you do and have done and mostly just for being who you are. –

Dana

Being loved is at the epicenter of all of our needs. Being loved by God inspires me to keep on. Being loved by my family reminds me that I am valuable even when circumstances seem to contradict that. Realizing the love of my friends is relatively new to me but already integral to my health. There is nothing more that I desire and my gratitude overwhelms me.

At this stage in my game, collaboration is essential and Dana has been a much treasured gift to me. You would have to know Dana as I do to appreciate her depth of intelligence, compassion and talent. Over the years Dana and I have been through many campaigns and there is no better way to get to know what someone is really made of. My life has been greatly enriched for having known her.

As always, Dana "delivered the goods" on this book and we all owe her a debt of gratitude. Thanks, Dana.

Being transparent is seldom easy, especially in a public setting. However, each contributor endured their inner struggles with courage and persistance to write words that revealed their authentic experiences, thoughts and feelings. I respect and appreciate each of them. Thanks, John, Dana, Casey, Mark, Heather, Steve and Dave!

Also, special thanks to Toni, Connie, Bob, Brady and my wonderful wife, Jean.

Paul

CONTACT INFORMATION

Dana and Paul have over sixty years of combined experience in training and communications. They've worked with companies large and small across the U.S. as well as in various churches and social organizations. If you are interested in bringing the message of God's purpose for us to your church or social group, please contact us at:

paul@evansonkeller.com or **dana@evansonkeller.com**

We can create programs and materials to meet your specific needs, or would be happy to appear as your keynote speakers for an event.

Our website is: www.evansonkeller.com

Paul Evanson & Dana Keller

www.ingramcontent.com/pod-product-compliance
Lightning Source LLC
Chambersburg PA
CBHW071510040426
42444CB00008B/1586